A Future with Natural Wood

Traditional and Scientific Facts about Trees

By Erwin Thoma

Translated from German into English
By Iris Detenhoff

Published by Moontime Diary

1. Edition in English 2015

Copyright © 2015 by Erwin Thoma and Moontime Diary, Australia

ISBN 978-0-9873172-8-5

Published by

Moontime Diary
PO Box 1200
Mullumbimby
NSW 2482 Australia

+61 02 6684 2770

moontimeoffice@gmail.com

www.moontimediary.com.au

All rights, also the partial copying or reproduction of an image and text, are reserved. The work including all its parts is protected by copyright. Any use without permission of the publisher is inadmissible. This applies particularly to duplications, translations, microfilming and storage and processing in electronic systems.

Credits:

Photos:

Cover Photo: Dreamstime

Cover Design: Iris Detenhoff

Color Photos:

    Demel/Kalchschmied

    Photo Studio Brigitte

    Erwin Thoma

Graphic Design:

    Ernst Muthwill

    Helmut Huber

Literature references:

Clausnitzer, Hans-Dieter, 'Historischer Holzschutz', Zur Geschichte der Holzschutzmaßnahmen von der Steinzeit bis in das 20. Jahrhundert

'Traditional Wood Preservation 'History about wood preserving methods from the time of Stone Age until the 20th Century;

Publisher: Oekobuch Verlag, Staufen via Freiburg 1990).

Leiße, Bernhard, 'Holz Natürlich Behandeln', Oberflächen im Haus färben, schützen, pflegen

'Treating Wood Naturally', Stains, Protection and Care of Wood

Publisher: C.F. Müller Verlag, Heidelberg and Aembik Verlag, Braunschweig, 1994

Weissenfeld, Peter, 'Holzschutz ohne Gift?', Holzschutz und Oberflächenbehandlung in der Praxis

'Non Toxic Timber Preservation', Practical Timber Treatments.
Publisher: Ökobuch Verlag, Staufen bei Freibuch, 1988

Table of Contents

Foreword by US Architect Gordon R. Pierce 1

Annotation by the translator 3

Prelude 5

Introduction 8

    A blind man identifies different types of wood 9

    How can a wooden chimney withstand fire for 400 years? ...11

    The sparkling eyes of a ninety year old 12

    A never ending friendship 16

Part One - 'Moon Wood' 19

Chapter One - Tension free, straight and stable - Timber harvested at the right time 20

    The replacement beam 21

    Swiss pine—a strange type of wood 25

    Insects are just not interested in those spruce and larch trees 27

    Beech trees which don't split or crack 31

    'Abbrandlerhoefe' - farms which have been rebuilt after a fire 33

    The merging floorboards 35

    Flowing water and the sign of the moon 37

    Wood and glass - the hour of truth 40

Chapter Two - Mature trees, the right place and aspect 43

    Matured in the forest 44

    How does wood come into existence? 45

Dense fiber grows at high altitudes 46

The natural forest 47

The distinct twins 56

Following Stradivari's footsteps 59

Two brothers standing at the abyss 60

Chapter Three - Moisture levels in wood 64

Musical instruments and moisture 64

How much moisture is appropriate? 65

Tree top pointing downhill and the forces of nature 66

Dry rot and wood rot 67

When is it useful to use the kiln? 69

Part Two - Man and Tree 70

Chapter Four - Toxic Wood 71

The biggest mistake in my life 72

Why toxic wood is a concern 72

A clear objective 75

What does 'chemically treated wood really mean? 76

The art of building natural furniture 80

An open question 84

Wood outdoors 85

Tourists, sharks and wood preservation 86

Chapter Five - An excursion into the world of healthy building and living 89

The building site - the size of a wooden cube 90

A breathing filter 92

Heat a family home with two cubic meters of firewood
through winter 93

'Holz 100' - the building solution 95

The master carpenter, bathrooms and wooden floors 105

The eternally dusty stairway 107

What is more hygienic? 109

What emits radiation in a home? 109

Chapter Six - Our forests are our best bet 111

Alternatives to fossil fuels 112

Waste - an unknown word 113

Fossil fuels and throwaway society 115

Forests sustain us with energy and clean air 120

Two villages are firing up 126

Chapter Seven - 'New' ways to live in harmony with
nature 130

The voices of science 131

Regulations, laws and dogmas 132

A sign post to a positive development? 133

The mystery of trees 136

This brings us to the conclusion 139

Part Three - Information and Service 140

Wood - a very peculiar material 141

Expansion and shrinkage of wood 141

Questions you should ask when buying wood 144

The best times for harvesting trees 150

Natural wood protection 152

What actually do we need to protect our wood from? ...153

Natural wood preservation to prevent fungi 154

Natural wood protection against insects 160

Timber constructions outdoors 163

Maintenance and care for wood 165

Sun and wood 166

Rough sawn or dressed? 169

Networking 171

The author's epilogue to this edition 172

Foreword by US Architect Gordon R. Pierce

Wow. *Definition*:

> Exclamation: expressing astonishment or admiration
>
> Noun: a sensational success
>
> Verb: to impress and excite (someone) greatly

This informal word best expresses the reaction I share with all those who understand and appreciate the significance of Erwin Thoma's creation – Holz 100. In this, his first book translated into English, you will find interesting and amusing stories that reveal Erwin's wealth of knowledge regarding trees, forests and wood. Perhaps, for some readers, this book will contain more information than they imagined possible for such subjects. For others, this will be a welcome introduction to wood-related subjects and an inspiration for a future using natural wood. Written in a colloquial style, it offers an insight into his humble genius.

For any advocate of environmentalism, this book should not only help clear up those myths regarding the use of wood as a building material but also reinforce the fact that this totally sustainable, natural resource, when used responsibly, is the best alternative to all other construction materials.

As an architect, I wish to highlight one aspect of this book that explains the remarkable building system invented and manufactured by Erwin that has won numerous awards and a loyal following in Europe.

I met Erwin for the first time about ten years ago. I heard about his company that manufactured a structural building system using 100% wood. It was advertised to have no glues, toxic chemicals, resins or mechanical fasteners. It was so well engineered that one could build multi-story buildings out of it or construct a single-family house in only days, not months.

Then I began to learn about the rest of the "wow:" the thermal mass of the product providing comfort to the occupants while greatly reducing energy costs; persons with allergies could live in these buildings without suffering from hidden toxins or allergens; sound attenuation was remarkable; hotels and spas built from this material were receiving rave reviews from guests who slept better, were more relaxed and enjoyed the smell of the forest unique to Holz 100 buildings. Finally, I learned that the manufacturing process was equally astonishing in that it recycles its waste wood in special clean-burn furnaces that, with supplemental solar panels, create more than enough electricity and heat to operate the facility.

So here I was introduced to a major structural building system based on ancient construction techniques, using state-of-the-art technology, and with a totally sustainable source of material as its basic ingredient – produced "off the grid" no less. This is truly the ultimate "cradle to cradle" product.

I expect to see this wonderful system produced in the United States in the coming years as its unique qualities – described thoughtfully and passionately in these pages – comes to the attention of builders, developers, architects and homeowners looking for the ultimate green building material.

Gordon R. Pierce
Architect

Annotation by the translator

When I think about trees and forests I am taken back to my childhood and my home among the Bavarian meadows, creeks and woods close to Munich. I remember roaming through local forests, climbing trees and looking for salamanders under moist logs. I remember the smell of freshly cut trees in the cold winter, the stacked piles of logs at the roadside, the feel of rotting wood turning to mulch in my hands.

Nowadays I live in Australia and publish a yearly moon diary which helps people tune their activities to the lunar cycles throughout the yearly seasons.

On a trip back home, I had the opportunity to listen to a talk by Erwin Thoma at a Timber Industry Conference in Wolfsberg, Austria. Afterwards I approached him with more questions about the moon and wood. It was a wonderful meeting of kindred spirits.

Since then I have read his books and visited the Research Centre in Goldegg and the saw mill in Gusswerk. I strongly feel his knowledge needs to be kept alive and made available to the English speaking population. I am glad to have had the opportunity to translate Erwin's first book into English.

I wish you joyful reading, contemplating and planning your future with natural wood.

Sincerely yours
Iris Detenhoff

Dr. Erwin Thoma

Ode to Wood by Pablo Neruda

Oh, of all I know
and know well,
of all things,
wood
is my best friend.
I wear through the world
on my body, in my clothing,
the scent
of the sawmill,
the odor of red wood.
My heart, my senses,
were saturated
in my childhood
with the smell of trees
that fell in great forests
filled with future building...

Pablo Neruda, Chilean poet and diplomat.

Born 1904 in Parral, Chile, Pablo Neruda died in 1973 in Santiago de Chile.

Prelude

Regardless of whether you are interested in building with wood, toys or furniture, this book will give you a better insight into nature's laws and traditional lore. You will find out how our ancestors managed the forests within the yearly seasons and cycles and how you can use this to your best advantage.

It will also be of interest to parents who want their children grow up healthy and free from allergies and asthma. Chemically treated wood can be the cause of severe health problems and also turns wood into toxic waste which poses disposal problems.

To use natural, untreated wood could be the answer to many concerns. It also can be of great assistance to the building industry to develop a healthier way of building. It would have a positive impact on global problems like forest decline and dieback. The consumption of fossil fuels would drop dramatically and allow us to have a new look at a healthy lifestyle more in harmony with nature.

There are people who determine the best days to harvest wood by looking at the 'moon' phase and position. Are they just dreamers or is there is something worthwhile to this traditional approach, something which can reveal answers to our very real and urgent questions today?

Is it possible for an average family to live in a solid wooden home, one that is untreated and free of any chemicals and glues? It is, because wood, the most unique and used building material, has qualities we don't believe are achievable.

It is important that we see trees not only as the next target of exploitation, but that we learn to use and maintain our forests responsibly. We need to make sure the forest soils remain healthy and balanced to grow at least as many trees as we take out.

Finally, I would like to thank my friend Iris Detenhoff. Without her deep interest in nature and her enduring commitment, this English translation would never have come into existence.

My thanks also go to Gordon Pierce, who as an experienced architect in the United States stands up for our forests.

I wish you much joy reading about the mysteries of trees.

Yours naturally

Erwin Thoma

This book has three parts

In the first part – 'Moon Timber'– you will find out why some wooden buildings are more than 500 years old and still in good condition even though half a century ago, there were no modern, high-tech chemical wood preservatives available. I will also tell you about an old, well-used wooden chimney which has never caught fire in 400 years. You will read about wooden boards which are not shrinking and methods used by the most famous instrument builders of all times. You will also find out why wood beetles are just not that interested in this particular wood.

The second part of this book – 'Man and Tree' –explores our modern and technical everyday life. It offers ideas about chemically treated wood versus ecologically healthy and sustainable building materials. You will find out how we are able to cover our energy needs by using our forests wisely. You will also learn about the circulation of energy and the mystery of trees.

In the third part, I discuss technical issues. You will read more about working in harmony with the seasons and cycles of nature. For those of you who are keen to experiment, there is more information about the best time for cutting, drying and working with wood as well as surface treatment

Dr. Erwin Thoma

Introduction

- **How a blind man identifies different types of wood**
- **A 400 year old wooden chimney that never caught fire**
- **The sparkling eyes of a ninety year old**

A blind man identifies different types of wood

The next time you are in a show room that features wood products, try the following experiment. With your eyes closed, slide your hands across a maple table top and then use the tips of your fingers and feel the rougher pores of ash or oak wood. Try this experiment outdoors on the hard wood of an oak or beech tree and then the soft wood of a spruce. There are many ways to discover the secrets of different wood species however mostly we rely on our eyes of course.

One day, a blind man named Andy was led into our house by his wife. With his stick, he detected steps, walls and corners while his wife made sure there were no surprises obstructing his way. After a short introduction, we all sat down at the table when I noticed that his hands were discovering and inspecting our well-used and smooth maple table top.

The couple was looking for a wood floor for their new house. The main issue was the type of wood that was to be used. But how is someone without sight going to choose the type of wood he preferred?

As this question posed itself, even our children were curious and joined us around the kitchen table. Only the dog wasn't impressed and kept snoring comfortably on his blanket.

Throughout his life, the blind man had sharpened his other senses more than a seeing person would be able to do and thus compensated for his blindness. With wood however, he was inexperienced and his finely tuned sense of touch, hearing and smell was discovering new territory.

Interested and excited he wanted us to explain every type of wood. All the time, his fingers, palms and finger nails were exploring the different wood samples we presented.

A unique atmosphere filled the room. We all felt him experiencing and discovering a world so new to him. Even our three children became quiet and fascinated by the investigative movements of his hands.

It was late at night when our visitors left. Both were satisfied with their choice of different wood for use in their hallway, lounge and bedrooms. The floors were to be pre-fabricated in our workshop from spruce trees, beech and oak.

About a year went by before they both returned. This time, his wife, Andrea, moved him swiftly through the house to the kitchen. Without much ado but with some 'cheek' he confidently identified and explained every type of wood we laid out for him to touch. Even an old carpenter with good eyesight couldn't have been more accurate. Gaping with amazement, it took me a moment to close my mouth.

Andy deserves a big thank you because he showed me yet another way in which wood touches our senses, influences and accompanies us every day, unbeknown to us. He strengthened my resolve to leave wood untreated or use beeswax or natural oil only in areas of heavy traffic. Timber preservatives and all treatments which close its pores prevent our senses from deeply appreciating wood, this wonderful and sustainable resource.

Touching any wooden surface always uplifts me and I consciously run my fingertips along the surface to 'sense' the wood. I allow this feeling to flow from the palms of my hands into and through my whole body. This sense of wellbeing is always the strongest when it comes through nature.

I invite you to be open to new experiences and allow yourself to be in awe like children are. The amount of effort this requires is tiny and yet the rewards will be well be worth it.

Make sure that as many purchases as possible are made from natural materials, materials you want to spend your life with. Smell and touch these things curiously and free of hesitation, like a child. Cloths, furniture, floor, wall surfaces and other items are all sources of energy and support.

How can a wooden chimney withstand fire for 400 years?

An old wooden chimney made a huge impression on me during my childhood. This strange object was located in a 400 year old farmhouse in the Austrian alps and belonged to friends of ours that farmed this mountain side.

The charred wooden chimney started above an open fireplace at the main floor of the house built from wooden beams. The black chimney flue made from larch wood boards went through the ceiling, the 2 bedrooms upstairs passing through and beyond the shingled roof.

This old farm house was perched like an eagle's nest upon the highest rocks above a steep meadow, close to my home town 'Bruck am Grossglockner'. Little did I know how the secret of this masterpiece was going to influence and shape my life. Years later, when my attention focused on the daughter of this family, I came across this wooden fireplace again.

There was another incident which made this fireplace so memorable for me as a six year old. If it weren't for the awareness of a farm hand, I might have burned down a hay shed and the farm too!

The penitential pilgrimage afterwards led me from the village police to my mother, from there to my father, to the teacher and to the principal.

At every stop, I experienced another interaction which was meant to deter my boyish brain from ever playing with matches again. The resulting success is obvious – I never forgot the prank and I still remember why this wooden fireplace never caught fire! The reason was: the particular larch trees which were used to build it were cut at a very specific time according to the phase of the moon. I found this very intriguing and practical at the same time.

The sparkling eyes of a ninety year old

This story has been told by our grandfather who lived in 'im Pinzgau', the area around Salzburg in Austria. Between World War I and II he worked as a carpenter six days a week from dawn to dusk. Here is the story in his own words:

"The trees were always felled in winter! You see, if you log a tree in spring, when the sap is pumping, the log contains heaps of moisture and nutrients. The wood won't be good for building because it warps, attracts fungi and termites. The best time to log trees is in winter when the tree is hibernating. The even better days are when the moon is waning and just before New Moon in Capricorn which falls around Christmas and mid-January every year. This wood has the least sap and moisture content; it will dry more evenly, won't warp and won't attract fungi and wood bugs.

"After the trees were felled, it took several months before they were further processed. Many of our building sites didn't have any access by roads, like the farmsteads and small alpine cabins high up in the mountains. We needed to be inventive and help ourselves with what was available.

"Yes, yes, these were long days… But then, no one was fussed about the tempo of our work. There was no rush. We steadily worked along with our hand tools.

We were eight men who went into the mountains in spring to build a shelter at the 'Windbachtal' (an uninhabited valley high up in the Alps of the 'Hohen Tauern'). First we put together a shelter made out of tree bark. We slept there at night until we finished a little cabin.

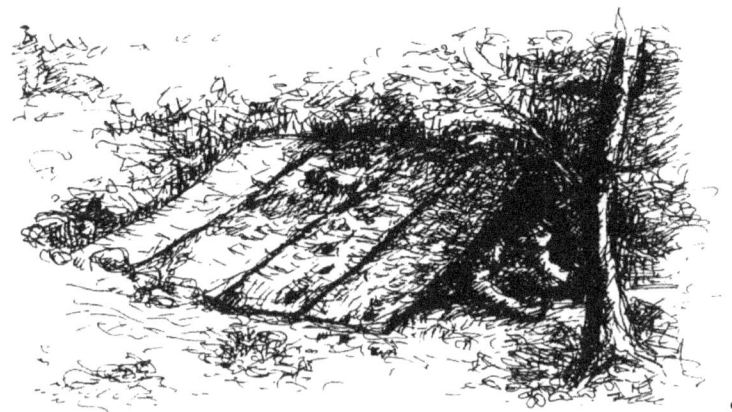

Simple huts made of available tree bark were the first shelter for carpenters in the Alps.

"After settling in, we built trestles from round wood. On those trestles, we processed the trees which had been cut down and prepared the previous winter. The trestles were placed at the side of the hill in a way that allowed us to lift the heavy tree trunks with our hand tools onto the trestle and lock the trunk into place. Then we used a colored string to mark lines on the tree trunk.

"A wooden frame with a saw blade tightened to it was run by three men. One man was standing on top of the tree trunk and two men were standing below the trestles. This gang of three sawed one plank after the other, in a steady and rhythmic way, for weeks and months until all trees felled were transformed into wooden boards and beams.

Cutting boards with a gang saw.

"The boards for siding and floors were stacked for several weeks to dry. They were tongued and grooved and dressed all by hand. The width of the boards was always determined by the tree, never by us.

"Most of the time we squared the beams with an axe which meant more waste, but no one was worried about this in the remote valleys of the Austrian Alps and we were much faster handling the axe than the saw."

When asked if he was ever injured, Granddad answered: "No. I don't really know why, but I have never seriously injured myself in my whole life. It did happen that someone hit his leg with an axe once in a while, particularly when we were hacking for days and weeks. Those injuries were treated on site with tree resin, sulfur and lard, Arnica and other herbs. Everyone usually recovered very well; some carpenters did end up with a limp though."

"Yes, yes," Granddad continued. "To build a wooden house took about a whole year. Larger buildings took us longer obviously. Every beam and every board was handled countless times, chosen, scrutinized, examined and sorted...Our love, joy and pride accompanied our work every day."

"Who was looking after you and cooking?" My son asked. Granddad's eyes sparkled in his weathered face:

"I was the cook. I cooked the same 'Muasl' (simple meal made of lard, flour and water) every day in the same pan. It seemed the others were happy with it, otherwise they would have taken over from me."

Granddad's face always lights up when he shows and tells us about the builds he has worked on. They all have one thing in common: He and his colleagues didn't know anything about modern techniques, wood preservatives, enamels, glues and other questionable substances. However, those and many other buildings constructed centuries ago still exist. Nowadays, in our fast and transient world, they are like enduring sign-posts showing us nature's way.

I too feel fulfilled and appreciated when Granddad looks at the work our young ones do. He slides his old, sinewy hands across the wood beams and floors and his face is full of recognition and approval.

He was inspecting a wood home, manufactured in our workshop and his words were: "You did an impeccable job; I don't have any doubts about you! "This was the biggest praise and encouragement for all of us. Building with a combination of natural and modern building methods is a positive step forward.

Even nowadays, when cost effectiveness and standards are paramount, it is possible to erect buildings in harmony with nature. Those buildings are sustainable, free of chemicals and are able to return back into the natural cycle. They stay within budget and survive us for hundreds of years.

Dr. Erwin Thoma

A never ending friendship

During and after finishing my forestry studies, I dedicated myself mainly to native forests and wood. The old wooden chimney became an important symbol of a real connection and friendship.

Humankind and tree got to know each other very well over a long period of time. Both learned to handle each other and many secrets have been exchanged. Together we can master most challenges and much of traditional architecture is living proof. There are buildings which have endured centuries of wear and tear, some even have survived fires. However, they were never treated with toxic paints and preservatives.

The old Court Building in 'Sulz', built 700 years ago – still untreated wood

Man relies on trees not only for building homes. We find examples of this symbiosis in nearly all areas of life e.g., wooden bridges connect two river banks. Their untreated posts have been standing in the water, often for centuries, without polluting the waters with toxic chemicals and without rotting away.

Due to its color and texture, untreated wood furniture is highly individual and always one of a kind. Wooden hand tools are sleek, tough, gracious and light. Wooden barrels play a significant role in perfecting the ripening process of the wine or cognac stored in them.

How did the old masters know? The ones who produced wooden musical instruments, without which we never would have heard the most beautiful music?

Ever since we began collecting information about human life, we have found evidence of the bond between man and tree in the form of tools, buildings and other wooden items. Historical sources go back centuries and records show the best times to harvest trees is always in winter.[1]

This has been mentioned throughout Chinese civilizations, Roman antiquity and medieval ship-building techniques until the beginning of the 20th century. Caesar and Napoleon, the Roman historian Plinius, the French, German and Austrian forestry commissions preferred time for harvesting wood was in winter, ideally when the moon was waning, just before the new moon in Capricorn. This happens to be around Christmas/ New Year every year.

The close study of these historical sources also brings to light another point of interest: besides the right timing of the harvest, the correct and thorough choice of wood type for the job required is of importance too. Even the way the

---

[1]*Source: Clausnitzer, Hans Dieter: 'Historischer Holzschutz', Traditional Wood Preservation 'The history of wood preserving methods from the time of Stone Age until the 20th century; Publisher: Oekobuch Verlag, Staufen via Freiburg 1990).*

tree has grown and the different types of soil and aspects have an influence on the choice.

With the increasing use of chemical preservatives in the past century, man, the sorcerer's apprentice, has unfortunately forgotten about these traditional methods.

In the first part of this book, you will read about the detour it has taken me to properly understand the wisdom my granddad passed on in his simple words. Later, I will introduce you to the secrets of our mysterious forests and how to incorporate nature in an easy and healthy way into your daily life. Irrespective of whether you are just looking to buy some wooden toys, furniture, lay a wooden floor or build a wooden house, this book gives you basic knowledge about wood and its products.

Part One - 'Moon Wood'

The moon moves ocean tides, it influences the fertility cycle of women and animals and the growth of plants. Sometimes, it also prevents us from a getting good night's sleep.

I now want to illuminate the fascinating correlation between the moon and wood. By using several examples, I'll show how practical it is to consider our yearly seasons and the moon phases when harvesting wood.

In early times, everybody who was involved with the forest and wood knew this. However, today there is an imminent danger that this very valuable knowledge and skill will be lost. Let us remember and record it so we can pass it on to future generations.

Chapter One - Tension free, straight and stable - Timber harvested at the right time

- The replacement beam
- Swiss pine - a strange type of wood?
- Wood which insects are just not interested in
- Beech trees which don't split or crack
- The farm called "Abbrandlerhof"
- Floorboards growing together
- The hour of truth

The replacement beam

It was autumn 1988 and I was employed as forestry forester in the Tyrolean Alps, at the 'Karwendelstein' mountain range (close to Salzburg) when I was visited by a well-known architect from Munich. He was planning to build a house for his family and he wanted to integrate his ideas about healthy building materials with aesthetically pleasing design solutions. This meant wooden beam ceilings, a large gallery with solid beams, wide wood flooring and an outdoor patio all built with untreated wood.

He was aware that usually the wood used for this type of job would be composite lumber, glued together with adhesives(glue-lam) and for the outdoor patio, it would have been high-pressure treated and impregnated with copper chrome arsenic.

The architect knew however, that it should be possible to do the same jobs with untreated wood, if only one found the right type! He came to see me because he had heard about Moon Wood and that I at times was selecting trees for violin and instrument builders who traditionally used Moon Wood.

I too was familiar with wood which stayed straight and true like the very slow-growing and mature trees up in the high valleys of the 'Karwendel' mountains. Only the most experienced master violin-builders would seek to use these precious trees and the time chosen to harvest them is of utmost importance. It usually is around Christmas to early January when there is about two meters of snow throughout the valleys and mountains of my forestry district. "Impossible" was my first reaction. "At this time, the path up to the small 'Ahornboden' is too dangerous because of avalanches."

The architect insisted. After we compared those trees with some others in a different, lower altitude valley, he was sure that only the ones in 'Johannistal im Karwendel' were meant for his house.

He believed in the impossible and his thoughts were constantly preoccupied with the question of how and who was cutting those selected trees at this specific time of the year when the most dangerous avalanches were waiting to be triggered. His conviction and his burning desire were contagious.

This task increasingly fascinated me and I was looking to do this job with a professional wood cutting contractor. I couldn't send my forestry workers to hike up there for five hours in snow up to their bellies to get those few selected trees.

Where there is a will, there is a way, and I finally found a fellow forestry worker from the 'Salzburger Land' (the area around Salzburg in Austria), who took on the job. It was autumn when we finally selected the trees and the contract was signed.

On 7 Jan 1989 at 4am, the five of us (the architect insisted he and his friend were part of the party, the logging contractor, my dog and myself), started our tour. We evenly distributed the saw, axe, wedges and other tools into four backpacks. Then we strapped snow skins under our touring skis and began the nearly five-hour-long ascent into the white and snow-covered 'Johannis Valley'. The selected spruce trees grew between the small 'Ahornboden' and the 'Laliderwaenden'.

The moon was waning just before New Moon in Capricorn – according to tradition, the very best time to harvest wood, so we wanted to make the most of the day.

Two men dug up more than a meter of snow to free the tree trunk, so they could cut as close to the ground as possible and not waste any precious wood. One man was sawing and the other wedging. Wedging was particularly important because we wanted the tree tops to point downhill. At 3pm, we were exhausted but happy. We cut more than 30 spruce trees at the right time and location and had them positioned with the tops downhill. There were enough trees for the planned home. As if he understood the significance of this day, my dog sat on a tree trunk overlooking the felled spruces and waited for the return back down into the valley.

After a short break, we swiftly skied back towards the forestry house. The giant spruces were left behind, with their branches still attached. The tree tops and branches still functioned as pumps and drained the remaining moisture from the trunk. Our plan was to bring the logs down to the valley in May (spring in the northern hemisphere), saw them and allow the wood to dry naturally before building with it.

However, things were panning out differently. By the end of March, the architect had sent snow equipment to remove the remaining snow and leftovers from avalanches from the forestry roads, because the building dates were accelerated. He wanted to have the Timber / Wood to build with by the end of May.

A transport company took the tree trunks by truck to the sawmill. At the last run, the driver would have had to leave some trunks behind, because he needed to be on the safe side. The drivers, who deal with wood day in and day out, know exactly how much they can carry before they are overloaded. In this case, the driver decided to take all trunks instead of coming back to pick up the few remaining ones. He was surprised when he noticed that even with those extra trunks, his load was not as heavy as he had expected.

He asked me, "Forester, I have never transported wood that was so light! How is that possible?" I was thrilled, because it showed that we had good reason to leave the branches on the trees until March. A tree which has been cut down tries very hard to produce fruits and seeds one last time. When we leave the branches on the trunk, they pump out incredible amounts of moisture and the wood in turn becomes lighter. When the tree top is pointing downhill, gravity too supports the natural dehydrating mechanism and can reduce the moisture content of wood from 100% down to 40–50%. This method is the most natural way of drying wood. Compared to kiln drying, this is much gentler on the environment and economically sensible.

Back to the building site: I was horrified about the intentions of the architect to use the wood in May. Without further drying it was literally "green"! Against my experience and expertise, I gave in. The one who pays also has the say. By end of June the fresh wood had been used to build the house.

When they celebrated the ceremony, I was able to admire the fine work of the cabinet-makers and carpenters. You can imagine how closely I looked at 'our' wood and how surprised I was about my discovery: in the lounge area, there was one beam which was not 'ours'! I was dead sure! It had grown faster than the others and its branch knots were different too. I was sure about it and I needed to know. When the architect came over he explained: "The carpenter had sawn one of the timbers wrong and replaced it with one of his beams."

This in itself was not a disaster, I just couldn't help notice. It was fresh and green, without splits and cracks and as expertly finished as all the other work in this house.

I still feel grateful towards the carpenter as the story goes on. One year later, this particular beam had splits and cracks as thick as a finger. Six years later, when I visited this house again, it was the only one in the whole house that was split and had cracks. All other beams, which we took from the 'Johannistal' at the right time of the year and moon phase, were beautifully intact, even though they had been processed while 'green'.

I knew very well that the correct choice of wood and timing were of importance for the quality of the wood. However, I didn't think it possible for elaborate constructions like this large gallery to practically stay free of splits and cracks. Nor would I ever have thought the difference between 'typical' wood and ours would be as obvious as in the replaced beam.

I now had a greater appreciation of Granddad's particular and detailed descriptions. More of his experiences and insights were coming through all the time and I endeavor here to tell you as much as possible.

Something else I learned then: It doesn't matter how big a project, if you build a whole house or just buy a book-shelf for your unit, what matters is only how you do it and how we treat our trees. If we decide to work with nature and use simple and natural methods, then everything is possible in the wood-working and wood industry.

Three things are responsible for the wooden beams staying stable and true:

1) Select the right type of tree, wood, for the job at hand.

2) Cut the trees at the right time (winter, waning moon, Capricorn New Moon).

3) Store, dry and process the wood properly.

Swiss pine–a strange type of wood

Many years after the replacement beam story, I was preoccupied running our own wood mill. Together with my wife and our employees, I made some changes in the manufacturing process. For years now, we only used selected trees which had been harvested at the right time to produce quality building and form wood to manufacture solid wooden homes and floors. This we call 'Holz 100'.

Because of this harvesting rhythm, the wood mill has its most quiet time in autumn. The harvest begins again in winter at a particular moon. At those quiet times, we do repairs and maintenance work and also mill wood for farmers in the area. In this case the farmer doesn't sell his own wood to the mill, but pays us to saw it into boards and posts for his own needs.

On one of those beautiful autumn days, a farmer came along and arranged with me to cut a stack of Swiss pine for him in the next week.

Swiss pine is also called arve and grows way up high in the 'Hohen Tauern' over 2000m above sea level. This wood is famous for the exquisite scent of its aromatic oils. For this reason it is often used for flour and corn chests. The flour worm can't stand the scent of the Swiss pine and in this way, the flour is protected. The wood keeps its scent and the effect it has on flour worms remains for many generations.

There is something else which one should consider when using Swiss pine. It is a pine tree and as with all pines, its wood should be harvested and processed during the cold months of the year. If the round wood stays stacked for too long before it is being sawn, the warmer spring air causes it to turn blotchy blue under the bark. This stain is caused by a fungus and even though it doesn't affect the structural integrity, it devalues the beautiful wood.

It was uncommon for a farmer to turn up with Swiss pine in September. If there was no obvious need, no one would cut them in the hot summer months, particularly not such a large quantity! The risk of the wood turning blue in the hot and humid weather was too big. So I was curious and present when the first logs went through the saw mill the next week.

The beautiful scent of the trees wafted throughout the whole mill; however I couldn't make any sense of what I saw: the round logs didn't look as if they were harvested only recently. The abutting surfaces were tanned by the sun as if the logs had been stacked throughout all of summer.

The boards and beams which came out of the saw however were pristine white and crisp. No traces of blue fungal blotches and bark beetles at all. Both should definitely have been present if the logs were stacked in the woods or in storage during this hot summer. Only if those boards had been harvested very recently, could they be this white.

When the farmer arrived with his last load of wood, he let me into his secret: "Yes, me too. I am glad that the boards turned out so pristinely. I was really quite worried about it being damaged this last summer, it's been so hot and humid. The cut logs were stacked in the forest for nearly a whole year. We had so much work with making hay and nobody had the time to get the wood down the mountains."

I thought: "He is fooling me". "No, no, this is not a joke," answered the farmer. Now I understood – he had them cut last year on 21 December when the moon was waning in Capricorn. We too were harvesting trees for wood flooring on the same day last year, but we didn't test how long we could leave them up there. Our logs had been cut into boards in spring and stacked to air dry before the hot summer came along.

Because of these Swiss pine logs, we now had strong evidence that the moon and the harvesting time of wood had an influence on longevity and resistance to insects and fungus. We also came across larch and spruce trees which were not attacked by anything either.

Insects are just not interested in those spruce and larch trees

At Christmas in December 1992, a group of forestry workers made their way up to the 'Gerlospass', the passage between the 'Upper Salzachtal' and the 'Zillertal' (Tyrolean Alps), to harvest a number of spruce and larches.

The workers knew that those trees had been selected by me and that I specified a particular time for their harvest. The men were starting to wonder why particular days of the year were suddenly of such importance. When one said: "This Thoma guy, he is a forester so he should know."

The workers were not the only ones who were curious. The head forester too looked at me with a strange expression when I insisted on specific days for the tree-felling. I fully respected his opinion, however I did insist on having it my way. The only thing which was important for me was that the particular dates were adhered to. Therefore I was present on site, in the snowy–white mountain forest.

The harvest of the trees proceeded according to my plans and we finished logging at new moon in Capricorn and the impulse changed from waning to waxing.

Nothing extraordinary would have happened, if fate hadn't accidentally intervened. The forester was interested to keep the workers on for a few days longer, to cut more wood in the same area. To avoid any confusion, I made sure 'our' logs were stacked separately about 100 meters distance from the edge of the forest. The workers stayed on and kept felling trees which were sold to a wood yard.

The logging crew left the other logs about 80 meters away from ours. Both groups of sawyers were in agreement and happy to trust each other. No one was afraid that any wood would be swapped or accidentally taken away. A short time later, two meters of thick snowcaps covered both stacks and the logs stayed there untouched until late spring.

This year we had a lot of extra work with sawing all the trees we had logged in different areas on those days in December and again in January. It is true that logs lying for long periods with the bark still attached are an ideal breeding ground for insects and that dreaded bark beetle and I was well aware that my wood hadn't been debarked. However, my spruce and larches had been logged at the right time and I was confident and didn't worry.

When May approached, I did get a bit restless though and made regular checks on the logs. Every time I walked up there and checked, I was reassured and returned at ease. There was no trace of bark beetles at all (those beetles drill into the bark and wood and you can spot their presence by their small drilling dust mounds which appear everywhere).

In May, the local forestry forester and with some concern about the log stacks. He was responsible for not having any wood lying around that could trigger an infestation of these beetles. I fully understood his concern but also knew that we needed a few more weeks at the saw mill before we could get to the logs from 'Gerlosspass'.

Once the round wood has been debarked and sliced into boards, the bark beetles aren't interested in it as a feeding or breeding ground and the risk is mitigated.

I told Franz that if he found even one beetle in my logs, he was to immediately ring me and I would change all plans and send a truck the next day to pick them up for processing straight away. This agreement was perfect for me. I could rely on the critical eye of the forester and also save myself a couple of control hikes up the mountains.

What then happened was utterly amazing. The anticipated phone call from the forester didn't come. It was mid-June and hot days and warm nights announced midsummer. There was no doubt that by now even the laziest bark beetle was up and working hard.

On one of those summer days, I took the young couple whose house this wood was meant for to check on the logs. The owner was in the building industry himself and well aware of the circumstances. At the wood stack, I handed him an axe and we both looked very closely at and under the bark for any bark beetle infestation. Nothing!

About 80 meters away, some of the neighbor's logs were left behind. The same wood out of the same forest, on the same meadow stored for the same length of time and logged in the same month of the year – only at the wrong moon phase! His logs were greatly infested with bark beetles. One drill hole was next to the other, every few centimeters. All logs were affected without exception!

The only obvious difference for me was the different moon phase when they were harvested and maybe the selection of trees. It was not possible to scientifically explain why the bark beetle preferred his logs to mine; they were stacked just 80 meters apart from each other. From all those years of experience when I was looking after my forestry as a district forester, I knew that bark beetles have a very fine, incredibly accurate sense of direction and gustatory system. These insects easily pick the weakest tree from a thousand logs, the one which counters their infestation with the least flow of resin and immunity. From these observations I concluded that it was not an accident what I experienced with the two wood stacks on the meadow.

> The one who cuts trees around Christmas time,
> His house will be safe and fine.
> Around Fabian and Sebastian
> The juices start to run.

Of course, I had heard of this old country lore. I also knew from experience that wood logged in winter had different components and ingredients to the one cut in summer. Its natural resistance against fungus and insects is higher compared to the one logged in summer. However it was new to me, to find out the moon phase had such an influence on the Woods' resistance to insect infestation.

On the way home, I pondered whether to find scientific evidence for this phenomenon or just to be grateful for the lessons learned. It is possible to increase the natural resistance of wood to insects and fungus. It starts right in the forest when selecting the trees carefully and timing their harvest correctly.

Beech trees which don't split or crack

Beech trees are the ones forester love seeing most. In mixed forests, beech leaves make particularly good mulch and the trees' roots macerate the ground more than others do. Their roots go deeper than the surface roots of spruce trees and the magnificent mighty crown protects younger trees. This nurturing character trait of the beech tree gave it the nickname: 'Mother of the Forest'.

The wood is a light-reddish color, visually evenly and calm/quiet and because it is hard wood it is hard-wearing. However, there is one characteristic which makes it difficult to work with. Solid, untreated Beech wood is in constant movement like no other wood. It swells and warps more than all the other native Austrian Wood species.

Sometimes, I have the impression the energetic beech has given its wood too much power and tension. These were the thoughts I was pondering when I was thinking about using local beech for solid wood flooring and furniture. It was the same temptation or impulse that excites the mountain climber to climb the highest mountain tops which spurred me on to tackle the vigorous, hard and extremely robust wood of beech trees.

We trusted the tried and true methods we have used for most of the other native wood: we choose trees which had grown steadily (stress-free) on humus-rich forest floor. The time of logging would be right and the stacking and drying process would be naturally slow. Nevertheless, our floors made of beech gave us the biggest challenge and triggered countless discussions in coming years.

It happens again and again that carpenters jump out of their seats when I show photos of beech floors in my PowerPoint presentations. They cannot believe a solid floor made with local beech would ever lie steady and not move. It's only when I invite them to look at the floors that those skeptics are transformed into believers.

I remember this anecdote of the time when we logged the first beeches. I chose the trees in the northern foothills of the Austrian Alps. The forest floor was already covered with young descendants of beech, ash and maple trees standing in the shade of tall, old trees. These youngsters needed more space and were waiting their turn to grow into the light. Old trees had to give way by falling down after centuries of growth or by being harvested. The forest, the location and the trees suited my plans and I bought the trees. The time of harvest was worked out exactly and noted down.

A few months later, just after Christmas when the moon was favorable, my trees were logged.

For the forester and loggers this was new and he was present for most of the time. He never encountered a customer who insisted the trees be cut a specific time.

There is a marked difference between beech and spruce trees. When cutting the long logs of spruce to the desired length, one only gets to hear the sound of the chainsaw. This is different with beech logs. Here one sometimes thinks a thunder storm is closing in. It happens all the time that the tension-loaded tree trunk cracks and splits the stems lengths. Freshly cut and stacked, beech wood will crack and groan long after the workers have left the site. Particularly when the sun heats up moist logs, you can hear them crack and splinter with a sound reminiscent of loud thunder.

On those 'best wood days', my wife and children don't see much of me. I spend them in the forest and mountains and see how the selected trees are doing. I make sure the harvest dates are being adhered to and help out where needed.

Naturally, I was present when the time for harvest came for the said beech trees in the foothills.

Our beeches were cut by two older wood loggers; both of whom have worked in this particular mixed deciduous forest for many years. The older one was shaking his head when he greeted me at the location:" I have been harvesting Beech trees here for 30 years now and never experienced anything like this. We haven't done anything different but not one log has cracked yet! "With his broad hand he wiped the sweat and sawdust of his forehead and looked over to his colleague who agreed, nicking his head.

The forester was skeptical when he heard that I was planning by the moon phases, but now he was puzzled too. He sold many beech batches, but it never was it so quiet. You didn't hear anything and later the stacked logs were absolutely quiet too.

By the time they were piled up, dried and transported to the saw mill a few cracks did appear, however just a tiny fraction of what would have been normal.

At the sawmill we were elated. We knew that if we now stack and dry this wood properly, the wood would be calm. We actually were able to quiet tension loaded beech with simple measures and we were rewarded wonderfully calm wood for our projects.

'Abbrandlerhoefe' - farms which have been rebuilt after a fire

This is the name given to farms in the area of the 'Salzburger Land' which were rebuilt after a fire. Bringing in the harvested hay, especially the second cut which is called the 'grummet', always poses a certain risk and sleepless nights for the farmer.

In the hot and humid midsummer days when thunderstorms are brewing, farmers often have to rush and bring in the still moist hay before a downpour. This way the hay might not get soaked in the rain, however a much more dangerous threat to the hay barn and farm buildings is lurking: A bale of hay only half dry starts fermenting and in just a few short hours develops an incredible internal heat. This sometimes causes the hay to ignite all by itself and is called spontaneous combustion. Quite a few stately and very old farm houses have turned to ash and rubble in this way.

For most of the 'Salzburger' alpine farms there is an existing privilege. In the case of a burned down farm, the farmer is allowed to cut trees for building materials in the state forest free of charge.

Living and surviving in this harsh and steep alpine environment has always kept these people closely knit. After such a disaster, neighbors would work together and help the owners to log the trees and swiftly start working on the new building which was then called the 'Abbrandlerhof'.[2]

Time was scarce too. Large farmer families, including the farmhands and animals, needed to have a new roof above their heads before the next cold winter would descend from the glaciers and surrounding mountains.

Over many centuries, building a farm in a very short time was only an exemption due to a catastrophe. A farm was built for many generations to come, not just the grand kids.

A project of this kind and needed to be planned carefully and was worked on over a period of time. All the accumulated experience of farmers, talented carpenters and trades people contributed to a lasting building. Due to this tradition and attitude of our ancestors, we now have buildings hundreds of years old and still functioning.

The 'Abbrandlerhoefe' however, those farms which needed to be rebuild hastily after a fire and couldn't possibly be built that way. Harvesting hay happens in midsummer when the heat causes the fermentation of hay and its

---

[2]*Abbrandlerhof' the name for the newly rebuilt farm replacing the original farm which burnt down.*

combustion. Therefore building wood needed to be logged in the hot part of the year and often didn't even have time to dry properly. This does influences the quality and longevity of the building.

As far as I can trace it, all the well preserved buildings were built with slow and traditional methods. The minimum requirement was to cut the trees in winter while the moon is waning. Even better are the days just before the New Moon in Capricorn.

The merging floorboards

I remember the incredible story of a 60-year-old carpenter which I will share with you.

"Shortly after I finished my master builder trade exams, I started my independent career in my parental company. As young carpenter I was very enthusiastic about new and modern technical advances which were developing all the time and I didn't pay too much attention to old traditional ways of harvesting trees at certain times of the year. The development of our operations was going along with the fast technological developments of the times.

A local farmer visited us shortly after my exams, around Christmas time. "Carpenter, please build a wood floor for my hallway. I would like you to do this very soon. I have recently harvested the wood for it in my forest," and he showed me the trailer standing in front of the house, loaded with his freshly harvested spruce.

I was very surprised and explained to the farmer that this was impossible to do. Flooring boards need to have been dried before they are laid. It would be best if floor-boards can air-dry for a year or even more.

Green flooring boards keep drying after they have been installed, they will shrink and the floor ends up with large gaps. I didn't want to do a job which was going to look appalling at the end. The farmer was laughing and said:

"You are right; however it is different with the wood I brought you. Those spruce were logged at exactly the right moon phase and position. Carpenter, please don't worry, you can take on this job and I will pay you."

Now I was really curious and took on the job. The green round logs were sawn and dressed straight away. I still remember it was difficult to get them through the dressing machine, because the boards still contained a lot of moisture. Afterwards we didn't wait and installed the nearly frozen boards as the farmer wanted us to.

I have visited him nearly every year over the past 30 years. The floor is still there, exactly as we laid it. There are no gaps whatsoever between the floorboards. You couldn't even insert a razor blade! You really get the impression that the boards have merged together.

That was the remarkable story of an old Tyrolean carpenter.

Over the years, I have come to know many stories and reports where trees were felled in winter on specific days. In one story, these green logs, still frozen, were taken out of the forest and installed as barn floors. In this particular barn wheat was to be threshed on the floor. It is essential that the floor is tight and without any gaps because otherwise the wheat pours through the gaps.

However, if you find yourself thinking about using green wood for your floor in your house now, don't! We have tried again and again to uncover the secret of those jointless, green floors. What we've noticed is that all the successful floors we have come across have been installed in rooms where there was no central heating. For floors in heated buildings, the above method needs additional drying and storage time where the wood slowly releases its residual moisture. (Note the chapter: "Where kiln drying is useful").

Flowing water and the sign of the moon

Another story by the above mentioned Tyrolean carpenter appropriately shows the influence the moon has on nature.

He reports:

"One autumn, this farmer in the Tyrolean lowlands asked his son to go up in the mountains and install five wooden water troughs for the cattle which are staying up there in the summer months.

Those troughs are dug into the ground and positioned right at a spring or little creek so that the water flows over the rim filling the trough without the trough needing its own intake.

The son wanted to postpone this job because right on that day was a dance in the neighboring village. The father however insisted: "those troughs need to go into the ground today and that's that." His son then went up to the alp and after he finished digging in the third trough, he left and went dancing. He installed the remaining two troughs a couple of days later and was confident his father wouldn't notice.

It was after the snowmelt in spring when the farmer finally made his way up there. When he came back and asked knowingly why two of the troughs have been dug in later than he specified, his son asked surprised:

"How do you know, you weren't up there all autumn last year?"

"I just had a look at them", explained the father. "The three which you put in at the right time, are still filling up nicely with water. The other two however, don't have a drop of water in them. The water runs past behind and underneath the trough."

When the carpenter told me this story, it was clear to me why.

Dr. Erwin Thoma

The proper trough.

Water flows behind the trough.

When I was forester in my district at the 'Karwendelgebirge', I was looking after a wide work of graveled roads. Dirt roads always experience the biggest damage when we have heavy thunderstorms in midsummer.

I noticed then, that thunderstorms and heavy rains created less damage when the moon was waxing. Usually there was just some gravel debris to be removed.

When the moon was waning however, it seemed additional and unseen powers were released. The water gouges deeper ditches and trenches into the roads, landslides occurred more often and afterwards, much more maintenance and repair works were necessary.

The moon's gravity directly influences the absorption and the release of moisture in any being or object which contains water. While human, animal and plant cells absorb when the moon is waxing, the earth absorbs water and nutrients when the moon is waning and the earth releases moisture and nutrients when the moon is waxing. It is a perfect symbiotic process.

You yourself can try out these energies in other contexts as well. Wooden fence posts never should be erected when the moon is waxing. After the next frost they will loosen and decompose faster. Fence posts set when the moon is waning or new seem to sit tighter in the ground and also last longer. The ideal time to set fence posts is when the moon is waning and in an earth sign like Virgo, Capricorn or Taurus.

Professional carpenters can make good use of this gravitational pull the moon has on earth. A wood floor laid when the moon is waning doesn't shrink creating gaps and also makes less sound when walked on.

In a carpentry workshop in Salzburg I found a carpenter family where four generations worked together. Of course they only laid floorboards when the moon was waning: "My great grandfather has done this successfully and obviously we too make sure we use the moon phases to our advantage." Those were the words the young carpenter used to confirm the longstanding tradition in his wood workshop.

Dr. Erwin Thoma

Wood and glass - the hour of truth

On this wonderful July morning the sun is warming the outside walls of the little log cabin in the 'Hohen Taueren', where I made myself comfortable with pen and paper. The sun, wind and weather have colored the wood and blended the cabin into the surrounding environment better than any artist could ever have done. No one is annoyed by the fine cracks and as long as the roof shingles are kept in good shape, this cabin will still be here in a few hundred years. When exposed beams in a house twist and have fine cracks, it is more a matter of taste and visual appeal than structural integrity, because the load-bearing capacities are hardly affected.

If you plan to use large glass panels in a building, the need for absolutely stable and motionless wood becomes a matter of life and death. Any movement, ever so slight, would become obvious when the glass panel breaks. We have been manufacturing wooden elements for large glass panels for quite some time now and even though it has become routine, it still is important to design a home well when using glass and wood together.

One of the most difficult and most exciting tasks was proposed by a young family in 1992. They were planning a winter garden for their new family home. However, the design was different from previous builds by us. The architect had specified the largest size of glass panel that could be transported. Our frames were to house five-meter-high, double-glassed panels. The architect was aware of the challenge this posed. Any slight movement of the timber frame would put tension on the brittle glass and cause it to shatter. For this reason, the architect wanted to use engineered wood to be safe rather than sorry. He didn't approve of using solid wood at first. The home owner however was aware of the toxicity of most wood glues used in engineered wood products and wanted to avoid this in their new home. Therefore they were looking for solid timbers. the beams needed to be cut from large logs.

We eventually got the job for this building and went ahead in our usual manner. I went out and looked for spruce trees which were growing in good forest soil at about 1400m above sea level. The logging took place in winter, at the waning phase of the moon. It was stacked and dried the same way we always do it. The large glass panels were fitted with our wood and the family was happy with their wonderful winter garden. Not quite a year later, the building was finished.

Every expert knows that dangerous movements of wood in a situation like that happen in the first year and rarely later. By now, 12 years have passed, 12 hot summers with heat and 12 alpine winters with frost and snow on the glass outside the wintergreen. The five-meter-high glass panels still rest without tension on the wooden frame joists as they did on day one.

When I hold talks, I sometimes ask the question if any of the carpenters, joiners or cabinet makers is able to mount a five-meter-high glass panel on solid instead of glued laminated joists. Their answer is always hesitant, uneasy and negative. Have crafts people too lost their trust in this wonderful building material?

We only need to progress thoroughly, step by step and there won't be any need for toxic and harmful synthetic building materials or chemicals in any area of any home. Every builder should reflect on this.

The architect was so convinced by his success that he then decided to design more components for his house. It made the hair on the back of my neck stand up when I first saw his plans. The ceilings upstairs were built to expose and show the long and continuous rafters and the internal walls dividing the rooms were built up to the rafters. However, he wanted daylight to come through a transom window from the entry into the bathroom and planned a glass partition sitting on the internal wall. The fact that the exposed ceiling rafters were running through both, the entry area and the bathroom, didn't bother him at all. He went to the glassier and ordered a glass panel with an exact square cutout for the wooden rafters. A rafter with the intention to warp or twist is never going to be stopped by a glass panel. This glass panel too would splinter with the slightest twist. When looking at this construction, I just admired the clients trust in our beams and saw this as an experiment and a strange way of measuring the possible movements of our beams. After four years, this panel is still intact and in its place. The experiment can be called successful and shows that even for very difficult and challenging tasks it is worthwhile to consider the possibilities nature offers.

As important as it is to have stable and calm wood, the question has to be asked, if it is useful to demand this characteristic for all other cases (like furniture, floor etc.) as well. My answer is "no", because wood is a natural building material, it is alive and working. Particularly demanding requirements like motionlessness often lead to the widespread use of glue laminated products (e.g. engineered flooring) which result in huge ecological problems like toxic waste.

Chapter Two - Mature trees, the right place and aspect

- **Mature wood compares with fine silk**
- **Two 'Alpenhorns'**
- **Walking in Stradivari's footsteps**

Matured in the forest

If we were looking at the core of an oak tree which was 1000 years old, we would find that the core of the tree is indeed a thousand years old, unless the tree is hollowed out. Those thousand years have not passed without leaving traces. Resins, tannins, dyes and an array of different substances have been deposited in the innermost part of the trunk. These materials have been converted which makes the difference between a young tree and an old, matured tree.

Stradivari looked for the old, slowly grown alpine spruce. He was looking for wood which had finished this maturing process in the inner part of the log.

Growth Rings: Only the innermost core of a thousand year old oak is really 1000 years old.

How does wood come into existence?

Which part of a 2000-year-old olive tree has already existed at the time Jesus walked the earth? The development of a tree begins with the sprouting of a seedling.

Every year, the young tree is being covered by a new thin layer of wood cells. The growth is happening on the outer skin, right under the bark of the tree.

You can find out the age of the tree by counting the growth rings.

With a 2000-year-old olive tree, only the innermost part is really 2000 years old. The outermost and visible part has grown in the more recent years. We can see the growth rings when looking at a cross section of a cut tree. Every ring shows another year of growth (see graphic).

If you count those rings, you find out how old the tree is. A specialist can tell more about the quality of the tree by looking at the distance between the rings and how evenly they have grown. Finely grown trees with little space between the growth rings (e.g. pine, 1mm and less) usually are less prone to cracks and tension, more durable and therefore higher quality building wood. One can compare the consistency of wood with textures and fabrics one uses for garments. The finer the weave and tighter the stitches, the more valuable and precious is the fabric.

Dense fiber grows at high altitudes

The correct choice of tree (according to what it is going to be used for later) and the right timing of the harvest are the two main criteria when working with wood in a natural way. Both measures are basic requirements for straight, stable and long-lasting wood.

We will take a closer look at influences such as the right location in the forest and stress-free growth in the next chapter.

The most important type of tree for building wood in Europe is the spruce. You find this fast-growing tree in lower-lying areas in nutrient-rich soil with growth rings that have up to 3cm spacing between them. The same type of tree grown in higher altitudes produces a spacing of just a millimeter or even less between the yearly growth rings. This much finer structure has many advantages for building quality homes and furniture.

When looking at the distance of the growth rings, you can see if a tree has grown fast or slowly.

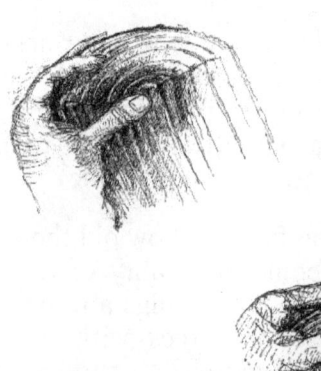

The finer and more interwoven a fiber structure is, the more elastic, smoother, tighter and longer lasting is the fabric. The very fast-growing spruce in lower altitudes compare to the fine fibers of high-altitude spruce trees like jute does to silk.

For this reason, we only work with very fine fibred wood grown in the Alps (approximately 3,000 -4,000 feet, 915 – 1220 meters above sea level) particularly when building projects with glass facades where the wood must not move or shrink.

The natural forest

A natural forest is another phenomenon which is important to the origin of the trees. Everywhere in the world Mother Nature had a particular combination of trees in mind which perfectly suited the location and harmonized with the soil. This forest family was best suited to the climate zone and grew abundantly. We still can find natural tree families in untouched and remote forests.

Even though we are now being taught about the importance of natural woods as part of forestry studies, it was forestry people who, in the past two centuries, have changed large parts of the middle European woods.

A very one-sided economic approach contributed to the conversion from naturally mixed forests to monocultures, of mainly spruce trees. Until the 1970s, University classes taught that spruce trees were the 'bread and butter' of the forestry industry.

The healthiest and best-adapted natural forests which have emerged over thousands of years were cut down in just one or two generations. What has re-grown since then are not wonderful mixed woods but sickly monocultures of trees foreign to the area and soil conditions.

You won't find any pure coniferous forests below the 3000–4000 ft. (1100-1200 meters) altitude and certainly not pure spruce forests. Coniferous forests with spruce, pine and larch trees grow best at higher altitudes such as in the Alps and in the northern European regions.

It took the forestry industry decades of planting monocultures before they began to realize that these unnatural plantings had many disadvantages. In a monoculture, the forest floor is no longer penetrated and infiltrated with a diversity of roots and the mulch produces mostly acidic soil. Those trees then become more susceptible to insects infestation, fungus, storms and heavy snow load.

The further away from its natural environment a spruce has been planted, such as warmer, low-lying areas, the more susceptible it is to diseases and pests.

Forestry management in Austria has learned this over the past few years. Today, a conscious and aware forester would not plant monocultures of trees which might not even be native to the area. Quite the opposite, today monocultures are being converted back into mixed forests.

Old roof shingles made of Larch. The wood turning grey effectively protects it from weathering.

Here the yearly growth rings are clearly visible.

Wood harvested at the right time, naturally dried and professionally crafted will last for centuries without being treated.

The sun's radiation causes the different effects depending on the orientation. The left side faces south and the right side east.

The Holz 100 system merges traditional and modern building methods.
Photo by Demel/Kachelschmied

It looks like a 'normal' Timber / Wood building however it is a Holz 100 building with solid 360 mm thick exterior walls.

Dr. Erwin Thoma

Our granddad skillfully used these simple wooden hand tools for decades.
Photographic Studio Brigitte

The traditional wisdom of our grandparents needs to be recorded and passed on to the next generation. As has been practice for hundreds of years, the old forester Fritz Loeffler artfully covered his stack with tree bark to keep his fire wood dry.

Dr. Erwin Thoma

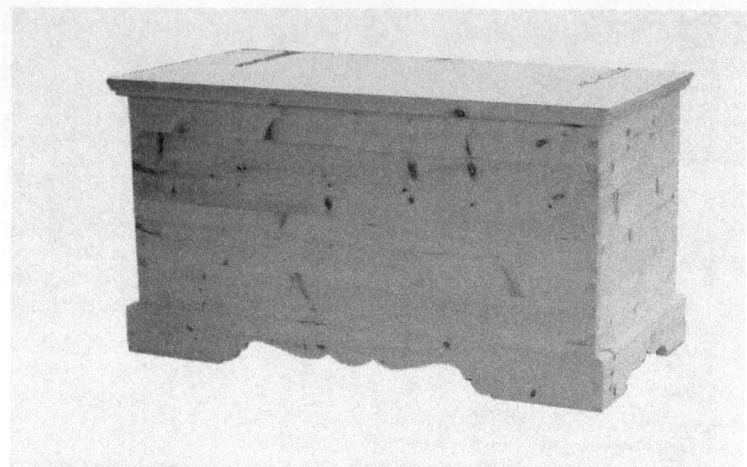

The scent of Swiss Pine repels insects from grain stored in this wooden trunk.

Parquet flooring made of cherry tree and alpine maple. All floors are made of Moon Timber.

A Future with Natural Wood

Hotel Waldklause

Hotel Urthaler

Due to Holz 100 technology, even large projects like hotels can be built with solid wood. Holz 100 offers fire safety, sound insulation, security and comfort at a level unmatched by normal building methods.

If one compares the end product of wood grown in its natural environment with wood grown in a monoculture, one can see the qualitative difference. A spruce grown in unnatural circumstances is inferior in quality and less durable compared to one which grew in its natural environment and conditions.

Taking this a step further, I would not use wood from monocultures in low-lying areas for a job like a winter garden or glass façade. The demands on the frame are high and the wood must be stable and calm.

I gleaned these insights from my experience of processing many thousands of trees from the forest to the finished item. The formula is always the same: observe nature and act accordingly.

To consider the origin of the wood is not only relevant to the forest owner or other wood professionals but also to the end consumer. Once you want to know where the wood came from, the seller will ask his supplier. Soon the saw mill and forester will be confronted and this will cause them to start sorting their wood accordingly. The end result of all these efforts will be buildings, toys, furniture and other wooden items free of chemicals and toxins.

We and the next generation need to take this opportunity to build a healthier and more sustainable lifestyle.

The distinct twins

Some woodworkers try to keep things simple and say dismissively: "Spruce is spruce, there is no big difference." However, individual differences between trees are caused by their individual location, composure of forest soil and climate. Those factors have quite a large influence on the growth and behavior of the trees fiber and structure, even in one and the same tree.

An alphorn builder from 'Salzburg' told me the following story. He found a large wooden post which fulfilled all his prerequisites and demands for building an alphorn. Good wood like this is very rare and he wanted to build two alphorns out of it.

This was his plan:

Indeed, he manufactured an identical shaped twin alphorn pair from the same tree. He used a device which guaranteed him identical radius, wall thickness and shape of both instruments. The only difference between both alphorns was: one horn's direction of blowing into was from the root to the crown and the other was from the crown to the root.

When he trialed both instruments for the first time, he was perplexed! The pitch of the instruments was markedly different!

Even though both alphorns were carved out of the same wood their sound was markedly different.

The instrument builder needed to make one of the alphorns several centimeters shorter to match the pitch of the other horn.

Sounds created with wooden instruments help us recognize the subtle interactions of wood fiber and vibration. The air column which swings 'against the grain' of wood sounds different to the one which swings with the grain.

The type of wood, its grain structure and the way we use it, all have an influence on the finished product. For the instrument builder, even the growth directions in one and the same tree are important. When building a house though, it is enough to look for trees that have grown in their natural environment.

Following Stradivari's footsteps

To build violins, cellos and guitars, instrument builders manufacture ultra-thin, very fine wooden lids. They need to vibrate freely without tensions, remain stable and not crack and of course sound great. These are the very particular requirements in order for the wood to be used.

As a forestry forester, I was lucky enough to work with some violin builders in my region. We often went out to look for the perfect sounding tree. For days we would search without much success. Then finally when we did find the one perfect tree, we felt exhilarated and blessed. After carefully noting down its coordinates, it was scheduled to be harvested at waning/new moon in Capricorn.

I never met an instrument maker who wanted to use fast-grown wood which was harvested in spring. They only consider the best and mature trees which have grown in high altitudes and were harvested at the right time.

The violin-makers often find their way back to our saw mill and look for violin wood. Sometimes they leave with a really good piece and are 'over the moon'.

Working with these experts and finding precious trees has provided me with great insights and helped me to persist when the road became hard and rocky. Once we reflect on the way most trees are selected and culled, anonymously and in large quantities, we start to question the direction the wood industry is taking.

We do know how we can increase the wood quality and reduce the need for chemicals. Here in the Austrian and Bavarian Alps we have plentiful quality wood growing to build healthy and lasting homes. Right now, more trees grow in our forests[3] than we are currently using.

Two brothers standing at the abyss

When working with natural materials or trying to understand human nature, we always need to observe and tune into each being anew and avoid generalizing.

The previous elaborations about spruce monocultures and mixed forests communities shouldn't lead us to the conclusion that all natural forests consist only of 'violin wood. In a human family, every member has different tendencies and skills. In the forest too, we need to find the best musicians for the orchestra, the most skilled people for trades, and academics for intellectual work and so on.

The following example of two Celtic maples growing right next to each other shows that they are not necessarily the same quality and grow

---

[3]*In Austria and Germany, only half of the yearly re-growth in forests is being used for manufacturing. The rest stays in the forests to provide shelter and nutrition for young trees. Just in Austria alone, it takes approximately two minutes to grow enough timber for a single family home! That would amount to 260,000 homes per year. If all of these houses were built, it would take 30 years to house every Austrian, from small child to old age in a solid, wooden house.*

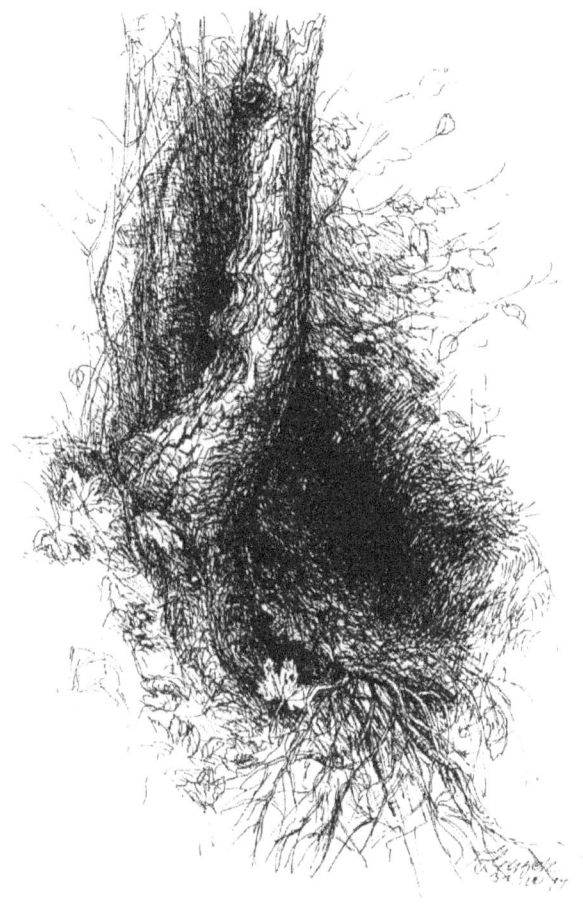

The trials of growing at the edge of a cliff are inscribed in the twisted grow of this maple.

These illustrations are the real drawings of two Celtic maple trees which both grow on the same cliff edge above a creek. To grow at this abyss, the roots which first held the sprout when it only weighed a few grams eventually has to defer the weight of a five to ten-ton adult tree into the ground. This load increases many times when the tree carries snow or its crown is bent by the forces of a storm.

The small tree grew into a structural wonder. No building engineer in the world is able to transfer the weight of his or buildings as ingenious as trees do via their root systems.

Its brother was luckier; a spruce tree (to the right) allowed it to grow straight.

The way the tree is rooted in the ground is a deciding factor for the straightness and growth of the fiber and its quality.

Let's look at the two maples. Both seedlings landed in a difficult location at the edge of the cliff. The increasing weight of the growing trees will cause the cliff edge to give way, therefore the roots and the trunks need to balance these forces. Through pushing and stemming, the fine roots spread and defer the heavy load of the growing tree into the slippery hill side or cliff. When they explore deeper soils levels, they carefully include any bump and little pebble. The constant nutrient exchange between roots and soil stabilizes and renews the forest floor even in initially depleted areas and facilitates growth.

The first maple tree has accomplished its job. It is deeply rooted, has stabilized the earth and keeps it from slipping. However, this struggle has left marks on the stem and wood. Even though it has grown in a tree community which is perfect for maple trees I would not use its wood for difficult tasks like long and wide floor boards or glass frame.

The second tree of these two Celtic maples was more fortunate. A spruce has grown just under it and absorbed the forces of the cliff edge. The maple was able to grow straight and free of tension. This stability and harmony continues to reproduce itself throughout the tree, up into its crown and results in the quality wood we like to use.

The art of forestry is about working with this extraordinary process instead of hindering it. Nature really doesn't need human intervention.

Chapter Three - Moisture levels in wood

- **Musical instruments and moisture**
- **How much moisture is appropriate**
- **The best way to dry wood**
- **Tree tops pointing downhill**
- **Is wood similar to a sponge?**

Musical instruments and moisture

The following story shows the importance of the moisture content or humidity levels on the drying process of wood.

An oboe player, who has become famous in Claudio Abbados' Youth Orchestra and works for several European concert and opera houses, has told me about his observations:

Oboes and clarinets are manufactured from black Ebony. Traditionally professional instrument makers used to store Ebony for 20 and up to 30 years before using it to build fine musical instruments.

In recent years the demand in Europe for these instruments rose steadily. This means that nowadays, there hardly is any oboe made of wood which has been dried and stored for that length of time. From the musician's point this is quite important, because instruments which have been manufactured of younger wood often end up with cracks and tears.

Just imagine how much saliva and damp breath these instruments are dealing with during a concert. Afterwards, the sensitive wooden instrument is being force dried by central heating which creates tension. Often the appearance of cracks destroys valuable wooden wind instruments.

New techniques like pressure treating wood with hot oil are being used to manufacture wood instruments. The Musician's comment was that these instruments look nice - and are not as prone to cracks, however their tone is different. Even though they are manufactured very well, they are only suitable for beginners and school purposes, not for the use in orchestras. This wood just doesn't sound right anymore.'

I don't play the oboe and I can't proof this musician's story, but it made me ponder anyway. I am thinking about the wood stacks which have been stored for years in our mill and remember business experts calling it 'dormant capital'.

However, the point is, when it comes to making the best instruments, slow and naturally dried wood cannot be produced by any modern kiln.

How much moisture is appropriate?

It is not only the growth of the tree which depends on water. The moisture content attracts fungi and insects which potentially cause damage to wooden buildings and artifacts.

The question is how much moisture is left in the wood? Below 20% moisture content, wood is protected from fungi and below 8-12% from insects. This natural resistance is the basis of wood preservation without toxic chemicals and the secret behind the durability of wood buildings which have survived hundreds and sometimes thousands of years without damage. 'Natural wood protection' means to harvest the trees at the right time and dry it in ways which further protects it from insects and fungi.

Trees or fresh logs contain large amounts of water often weighing more than 50% of the trees weight. Every piece of wood, no matter if it has been used for furniture, roof trusses, toys or building, contains only a fraction, approx. 6-20% moisture content.

In the following chapter you will read about the other requirements you need to consider to produce high quality building wood.

Tree top pointing downhill and the forces of nature

The old wood workers say: "If you want quality building wood, the best way is to cut the trees and have them lying with their tops pointing downhill for a few weeks before you cut off the branches."

Why?

When a tree is cut down, it wants to procreate one more time. The sap moves through the channel and pipe system from the trunk into the branches to grow leaves and flowers. When the tree is lying tree top downhill, gravity too supports the flow, naturally drains the sap and the trunk dries evenly.

We wanted to test this and undertook the following experiment: One spring, when the trees were growing leaves and the sap was moving freely, I cut down a beech tree. I cut the trunk into two pieces and had both pieces pointing down a hill side; one piece was lying with the tree top pointing downhill and the other piece with the bottom of the trunk pointing downhill.

When the tree top points downhill (right), the trunk loses moisture faster than the one on the left.

After a short time, the sap started to drop from both stems, however the piece lying downhill with the tree top lost three times as much sap than the other one, which had the bottom part of the tree pointing downhill. This is not surprising and confirmed our expectation. This ideal way of drying wood naturally results in a better quality product.

Dry rot and wood rot

The water in a living being like a tree is more than just content in a tank which can be filled or emptied. The example with the oboes shows that at the end, kiln dried wood contains the same amount of moisture as wood which has been dried for 30 years. However, oboes made from kiln dried wood crack whereas seasoned wood doesn't, it stays stable and resonates.

The ability of wood to absorb and release moisture can be compared to a sponge. Timber which has been stored for a long time matures and dries slowly. It stays in shape even when the humidity is fluctuating, whereas younger and kiln dried wood tends to warp and bend. This principle always applies.

However, wood used for building and furniture manufacture has shorter drying and storage times than the highest quality wood used to build instruments. Depending on the type of tree and intended use, one to three years of air drying are sufficient here.[4]

The rule to remember is: The faster the wood is drying the more it will warp and twist. This is called the sponge effect. It means that on humid summer days, this type of wood absorbs more moisture from the surrounding air, expands and works harder than wood which has dried naturally over some years.

---

[4]*You'll find a table with useful drying times at the back of the book in the service part.*

A stack of sawn boards which has been stored outside for a few years (protected from water), has been exposed to hot summer days as well as freezing winter nights. These boards have not only dried, they also experienced and adapted to the different weather conditions. This 'memory' has a relaxing effect on the wood.

In those years of storage and slow drying, something else and as important is happening: oxidation and several other processes cause the breakdown of nutrients for insects and fungi. This natural process to preserve wood is not happening when speeding up the drying process with a kiln (which takes from a few days to weeks).

Some economic experts who visited our saw mill showed utter disbelief when they saw a stack of oak boards which had been drying for four years. These boards were to be used for a solid wood floor at some stage. Four years of tying down capital when everyone knows you might as well kiln dry it in just a few days or weeks. How can you afford to leave this kind of capital lying around for such a long period?

From a business point of view this might seem right. However it doesn't have anything to do with using wood in the most ideal way.

The purely technical way of drying wood fast, unfortunately misses out on all the subtle benefits of working with nature. The resulting wood often needs to be treated with questionable preservatives or glues. Treated wood ends up as toxic waste and cannot be returned into the natural cycle to turn into valuable mulch and nutrients for other plants. It also cannot easily be burned either. This toxic waste is the beginning of a dead end road.

When is it useful to use the kiln?

With our middle European climate, the moisture content ends up averaging around 15–20%. Even in 100 years, it probably wouldn't be any drier.

Apartments with central heating have dry air with a moisture content of around 6–10%. Floor boards which have only been air-dried would lose the last bit of moisture, shrink a little and create gaps. In this situation it is useful to rest dry the boards in a kiln before installing the floor. However the natural drying process should have been finalized before the kiln.

Part Two - Man and Tree

The stories and experiences in the first part of this book give us an idea of how to appreciate and integrate nature's gifts into our lives. Often unaware, we humans take risks with our environment and our physical health because we don't really totally understand how to use and handle renewable resources in an appropriate and natural way.

It is time to wake up to nature, take note of her cycles and laws. This way we rewarded ourselves with a healthier and abundant life style.

A livable planet and healthy homes which source energy without harming the environment are not utopian ideals! These are the goals we are going to achieve with a positive attitude and a happy outlook. The second part of this book will tell you how you could accomplish this.

Chapter Four - Toxic Wood

- **The biggest mistake in my life**
- **Why toxic wood is a concern**
- **A clear objective**
- **What does chemically treated wood really mean?**
- **The art of building natural furniture**
- **An open question**
- **Wood outdoors**
- **Are we more scared of sharks than toxins?**

The biggest mistake in my life

In one of my talks a gentleman stood up and told the audience in his own words about the biggest mistake he ever made:

"I am working in the building and real estate industry and a few years ago, I built a house for my wife and me. This house had external wood cladding which was painted with some wood preservatives as was usual then. Two years later, my wife gave birth to our first child which is now physically and mentally disabled. We never tried to prove a connection between the wood treatment and the disability of our child; it couldn't make our child healthy either. However I do know now that treating the external cladding of our house was the biggest mistake I ever made."

Why toxic wood is a concern

Synthetic paints, chemical treatments and large-scale wood lamination turn wood into a mix of different materials and compounds. Their effect upon humans is mostly unknown and it is impossible for the average consumer to correctly gauge the risk they are taking with these products.

Why does the wood industry produce and install toxic building materials? Are authorities informed, not guilty or just plain negligent? Are chemicals really that bad?

Here an excerpt from the 'Salzburger Nachrichten' back in the year 1993:

> "Wood preservatives, two parole sentences"

> *Frankfurt Main (SN, APA). On Tuesday the Frankfurt "Wood Preservative Trial" sentenced both accused men to one year suspended prison term each and a total fine of 1.7 million Schillings, payable to several joint plaintiffs.*

The executive directors of the company XYZ, 64 year old XY and 62 XY were both sentenced guilty of negligent bodily harm, concomitance, the negligent release of toxins and selling toxic goods while being well aware of the danger they are posing."

Please, allow me now to tell you about my own personal motivation and why our family started taking toxic chemicals seriously.

After six years of living in the Tyrolean Alps in an old Timber cabin, we moved back to our home town in the area called 'Salzburger Land'. The cabin had been built of solid and untreated timber and the house accommodating us now was about 30 years old. It was built at a time when the words 'toxic' and 'building materials' were not yet combined. Nobody was suspecting that building materials are going to cause serious harm to anyone's health.

Our family was perfectly healthy until suddenly two of our children started coughing and having breathing difficulties. First without fever, later with a slight temperature rise, followed by asthma attacks, fear of going to sleep and cries for help at night: "Mama, Papa, why can't I breathe anymore?"

The first doctor didn't have a diagnosis but prescribed a dose of penicillin. The next doctor didn't have any idea either as to why this condition was persisting. He prescribed cortisone for our children and elaborated in their presence, how they would have to carry a puffer with them for the rest of their lives.

We needed a third doctor before we realized we couldn't expect any help from conventional medicine in this matter. This third doctor tested for allergies. Holding our boy's arm he exclaimed: "Oh my God, this boy is allergic to just about everything!" He listed a selection of native trees and grasses. Strangely, I am a forester and I have taken my son at pre-school age on many walks and tracks throughout the seasons and blooming times of the year, day and night, in and out of the forest and never found him to be overly sensitive to anything.

Our commonsense told us that those medical reckonings couldn't be correct. Our children grew up in the Alps with goats, chickens, dogs and cats. There were no allergies or any other symptoms. Our son in particular spent a fair amount of time in the company of our Billy goat. Apart from the goatish scent, we never noticed anything having a negative impact on him.

The health symptoms had appeared just after we moved into our new house. We thought maybe something in our new environment was having this effect on our children's quality of life. When looking closer at our new surroundings, we soon realized the house was playing a big part. The brick work was not insulated and therefore there were no dust or microfibers from mineral wool or emissions from plastic insulation. The wood cladding was not treated either and we ruled that out as a possible cause as well.

However, the floors were a different story all together. All the rooms had particle-board floors covered with carpets and vinyl. Particle boards are nothing more than wood shavings mixed with synthetic glues and pressed into boards. After realizing this might be the possible source of our troubles, we removed all chip and particle boards as fast as we could and replaced it with untreated and solid wooden boards from native trees like oak, ash and larch. There is no toxic wood in our house anymore.

Shortly thereafter, our children were back to their normal healthy selves. What a relief! Like the man who made the biggest mistake. We too couldn't find a 'scientific diagnosis' for the disease of our children. The most important thing for us was the result: Our children have their health back.

Just to think about how it could have ended if we had taken the advice of any of the doctors. If we were prepared to settle for an asthma puffer and not changed the floors of our home!

Just now, while I am writing these lines, our eldest son has come home from school and told us that he was the fastest runner today. I remember the times when he was ill in bed and I told him that every illness has a reason and how faith can move mountains. We all believed strongly that one day he would be running again like a deer in the forest.

The question: "Mama, why can't I breathe anymore?" cannot stay unanswered.

We know that our chances to supply clean air for all living things are actually quite good. Once we critically assess the materials we surround ourselves with, we will drop some of our habits and unnecessary demands. Turning towards nature doesn't mean loss of comfort or quality. Quite the opposite, we are healthier and feel better when we live in a natural, untreated environment.

After experiencing the illness our children went through and finding the solution, we were able to support people who had been suffering from allergies and doctor visits over the years.

Many families go through similar situations. The best approach really is to replace synthetics and treated furniture, floors, walls and ceilings with natural materials. When building or renovating, check all materials you are using and removing.

A clear objective

On our quest for an answer to our children's illness, we engaged not only our minds but we also followed our hearts and gut feelings.

We wanted our dream house to be built with only natural and untreated materials. Our chances to materialize these then unusual wishes were pretty good. We had our own little sawmill, my experience as a forester, the Alps surrounding us with good Timber and last but not least, the expertise of our nearly ninety-year-old grandfather. He generously shared his experience and wealth of knowledge as a carpenter and always had an ear for us.

The task at hand was clear: We wanted to produce straight, tension-free building material to renovate our home with. It had to be purposely selected and harvested at the right time. It needed to dry slowly and naturally. Furthermore, we were using grandfather's traditional techniques to make the building last for many centuries to come and without ever having to treat it with chemicals.

The answers we found on our search were ingenious and simple at the same time.

From roof trusses to a solar winter garden, a solid wood bed to the fence outdoors, there is not one area known to us which warrants the use of harmful chemicals. We just need to work with the wood in a constructive way. And the good thing is, this approach needs much less maintenance and is far more comfortable!

In a normal living situation with average dimensions and room sizes, you can realize your dream and choose untreated furniture to eliminate toxins in the home environment.

What does 'chemically treated wood really mean?

In the past few centuries, laminates, glues and synthetic preservatives have turned a natural building material into toxic waste.

A large percentage of modern wood products, furniture, building and flooring will be classified and treated as toxic waste. The same chemicals which turn wood into a toxic waste also diminish the quality of our lives and lead to questions like: "Mama, why can't I breathe anymore?"

Let's have a closer look:

The three main uses are:

1. Chemical technology: adhesives, glues and laminate
2. Surface treatment: laminates and paints
3. Preservatives: insecticides and fungicides.

After decades of unconcerned use and patronizing talk by the industry, we now see some treatments (with active ingredients like PCP, Lindan and adhesives containing Formaldehyde) recognized and declared as dangerous!

This only happened after many people had suffered terrible damage to their health and now Formaldehyde has been replaced by another highly questionable synthetic resin which has Isocyanate on its list of ingredients. It is hard to believe to see the devil being chased out by the deuce.

Clever sales techniques praise Formaldehyde-free furniture, wall and floor panels as healthy, natural and eco-friendly. But they forget to mention their adhesives contain Isocyanate.

Here is a quote from a personal talk I had with the head chemist of a famous natural paint manufacturer, Mr. Erwin Schusser: *"If you compare the toxicity of Isocyanate and Formaldehyde, you will find Isocyanates are definitely not less toxic....!"*

Properties of Isocyanates:

Isocyanates are highly reactive chemicals. They are used in large quantities for the production of polyurethanes.

Usage:

The use of polyurethane varies widely (mattresses, soft foam materials, sealants, insulation, adhesives, finishes and others).

Effect:

The toxicity of polyurethane mainly stems from the original and unchanged chemical compound Isocyanate. Isocyanates are constantly being exuded into the surrounding atmosphere and have a highly irritating effect on mucus membranes, particularly the respiratory system. Allergic reactions like coughs, asthma and other breathing difficulties and headaches often are triggered.

Toxicological rating:

Isocyanates are highly active chemicals which react with skin and mucus membranes. They are even more toxic than Formaldehyde. The replacement used in chipboard is Diphenylmeth and Isocyanate which forms Diaminodiphenylmethane. This compound is strongly suspected to cause cancer.

In a fire situation, Polyurethane is a death trap. Poisonous gases like Hydrogen Cyanide (Adler/Mackwitz: Eco tricks and Swindles, page 274).

Isocyanates are part of a particularly dangerous group of chemicals. Even small concentrations of fumes or dust (produced by normal wear and tear of these materials) in a room can cause serious health damage. Irritation of the mucus membranes to nose, bronchus and lungs leads to shortness of breath and chest pain. Under prolonged exposure spasmodic coughs and bronchitis are the result. Isocyanides cause allergic reactions, e.g., Isocyanate asthma, a lung disease (Katalyse Umweltgruppe: das Oekologische Heimwerkerbuch; Rohwohlt, S 152).

Substances which are suspected to be carcinogenic (aromatic amine amino acids) can be found in Isocyanate products and also are being released by them.

Even if it were possible to swiftly warn people about the dangers posed by Isocyanates and the chemical compound would be removed, more and more medical cases of Isocyanates toxicity would become public.

Precious time is passing by and in the meantime, the industry is looking for new chemicals to replace the current ones. The laboratories of the fossil fuel and petrochemical industry are developing new compounds with totally new molecular structures which are not part of our natural environment. Until it has transpired that those new molecules also prove a threat to the health of humans, more time goes by. I believe that it is an endless 'Catch 22'.

The wounds inflicted on nature by the production of synthetic products have not been factored in yet. Toxic treatments create toxic waste which cannot be put back into nature without causing more damage. It makes sense to use untreated wood for floors and cladding inside and outside. No one needs to take the risk in the first place.

Why are we following the dead-end road sign of the petrochemical industry? Why do we resolve simple woodworking steps with a sorcerer's apprentice mentality? Why would we inflict more damage to our health and environment?

If you wanted to prevent any chemical experiments on yourself, you should develop a healthy curiosity when buying wooden products. Prefer manufacturers and dealers who are open to disclosure of their product treatments and constituents. Someone who can prove the product is harmless to your health and the environment.

The art of building natural furniture

A manager who started to produce mass furniture in his factory in the 1960s and 1970s told me about the times:

"We were making furniture from a one-off piece to mass production. Those new chipboard panels were laminated with cheap synthetic decorations and mass manufactured. We knew that this furniture would not survive one move but they were incredibly popular. People bought them like crazy and we were making profits in the millions. Today I sit here as an old man and realize what really took place."

The conversation between us went on. Chipboard panels are nothing else than a hardened mix of pressed sawdust fibers and glue. This type of panel is still used today in the majority of cheap furniture. We talked about the fact this type of furniture can't be easily disposed of and nobody really knows how many people have been affected so far.

Plywood consists of three, five or more layers of thin wood glued together. For the top layer, visually perfect sheets are used, whereas the layers underneath are of a lesser quality.

Another type of panels is being produced with small wooden batons. Both panel types are quite advanced compared to chipboard, because the amount of glue used per square meter has been drastically reduced.

However, the main issue from a healthy building point of view is still the same: Wood is being mixed with synthetic adhesives and we end up with substances we don't normally find in our natural environment. Again, in a few years' time, we will probably hear more about people's experiences and health effects.

Chipboard

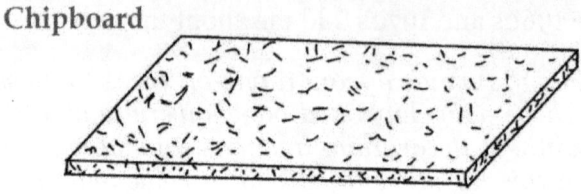

Plywood

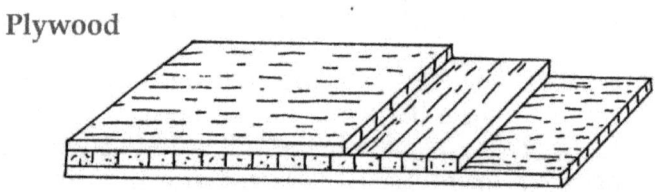

Engineered Wood Products

On the search for furniture without laminates and harmful adhesives, our family went all the way without any compromise. We found cabinet-makers who made our furniture to custom order using our own wood, which was harvested at the right time. The furniture ended up being wonderfully unique and will last for generations to come.

Dovetailed corners, wooden frames and paneling replace particle boards and laminates. Only for a couple of joints did we use a casein[5] glue to support handmade fittings.

---

[5]*Casein is a non-toxic milk product and compostable. It has particular properties like a long setting time and short shelf life*

It actually is very special to us that we know where each piece of furniture originated from and what it was made into, a table, bed or trunk. The inherent memory of the landscape where the tree has grown manifests in our lives and houses. Most people cannot share such an experience and we feel very blessed.

There is another point worthwhile considering when opting for individual solutions. Purchasing handmade furniture is a purchase which lasts for generations. The design needs to be practical and functional and it should survive short-lived fads and stay attractive. Experience shows that the best carpenters are not necessarily the best designers and it is worthwhile to consult a good and talented interior designer.

After having resolved all creative challenges, the artistic skill of a master cabinet-maker can produce the most divine and health giving furniture without any compromises.

Solid wood slabs and boards are used for higher quality and more expensive items. Considering the furniture was handmade and had a long lifespan, we thought the price was fair. However not everyone can go this way without some compromises and for a young family which is just starting their household, the price tag can be very challenging. It was sad for us to find many cabinet-makers and carpenters do not consider those wishes at all. This in turn causes higher prices and long waiting times with manufacturers who do.

What can someone do who can't pay a fortune? Is the only choice between cheap throwaway and expensive custom-made furniture? No!

---

once it is mixed with water. This kind of glue is mostly used by tradesmen working with hand tools. It is not used in mass production.

The crucial point here is to avoid chipboard and plywood. Where possible, use solid wood elements and if necessary, fasten the boards together with dowels instead of adhesives. Use paints that are plant and oil based and waxes which are recommended by biological building standards and have all ingredients declared.

We had a very good look at the serial production of solid wood furniture and found examples which were reasonably priced. From a financial and a building biologist point-of-view, mass-produced solid wooden furniture ranked very well.

The advantages customers have when they buy mass-produced wood furniture are known prices, fast and simple purchase and swift delivery. The design is a matter of taste but usually the customer receives a better, more practical piece than they normally would when they shop for a custom-made piece.

We need to recognize that most furniture will be landfill in a few years from now. Your investment in craftsman-made solid wood furniture will last for many generations and ultimately contributes to your own well-being and a healthy intact environment.

PVA glue

Customers who are concerned about glues often hear sales people say: "We only use PVA glues– there is no off gassing of formaldehydes."

PVA glues consist of poly Vinyl acetate which is dissolved in water. Different additives are added to speed up the curing process or increase water resistance. Compared to Formaldehyde or Isocyanate-containing glues, PVA glues are a huge and positive step forwards.

It has to be strictly stated though, that PVA adhesives and their additives are not substances occurring in nature but are synthetic products made by the petrochemical industry with all the disadvantages in relation to energy consumption and environmental health.

The problems with 'new molecular structures' (new as in our bodies have not been exposed to them yet) which have been discussed earlier, apply to PVA and its additives as well.

From an ecological and biological building point-of-view, we can sum up the above:

PVA is less hazardous for the climate indoors than synthetic adhesives. So far there are no known health hazards. However the production of PVAs by the petrochemical industry has serious environmental disadvantages.

If in doubt, always opt for furniture which contains the least adhesives.

An open question

People who read trade statistics can find out about the yearly import of cheap chipboard containing Formaldehydes. Many millions of square meters are imported from the former eastern bloc countries into the west. I just cannot figure out, what all this imported chipboard is being used for or where it is dumped. There must be a gigantic hole somewhere in Austria, Germany and other west European countries where it all ends up. Or is it being sold as locally produced and formaldehyde-free panels?

Where is the hole in which all the imported formaldehyde chipboard ends up?

Wood outdoors

Timber treated with insecticides and fungicides for outdoor use are often used in sensitive areas such as playgrounds and vegetable patches.

There are two different ways to impregnate:

1) From a biological building point-of-view, boric salts are harmless but rarely used. This treatment doesn't make much sense for outdoors because the salts are being washed out fairly fast and are only protective for a short time.

2) Synthetic chemicals such as insecticides and fungicides on their own or in combination with salts. One variation, which often is thought of harmless, is the treatment with chromium salts. However, trivalent chromium is suspected to be a carcinogenic. Synthetic preservatives turn wood into toxic waste and pose severe health threats to humans, animal and environment.

This has triggered reactions from the population and city councils. More and more communities refuse to use wood treated with poisonous heavy metals for their play grounds and this is a good development. Their reason is that the expected cost of disposing of this toxic wood would be too high! I keep wondering why their first and utmost concern isn't the health of the children.

The interesting bit of this story is:

Outdoors, untreated wood from slow-growing trees such as alpine Larch, Oak and Robinia will actually last and even outlast treated pine or spruce. We actually arrive at the same goal without the use of preservatives.

Tourists, sharks and wood preservation

A shark attack in the Mediterranean summer season would receive sensational reports by the press. They would discuss at length the danger of sharks for the umpteenth time and many people would instinctively perceive the danger.

Why? We have learnt to be aware of dangers which have been known to us for the past 20,000 years of human history. To be eaten by a big animal is one of the dangers which have always threatened us and we have adjusted to that not only mentally and physically but also instinctively and emotionally and specific protective reflexes are being passed on to the next generation to stay clear of shark, wolf and bear.

Human behavior studies show that it takes a very long time for new protective reactions to anchor in our DNA and a few generations are just not enough. Rotten meat for example, has always existed and for generations we have been protected by our genetic information. We all have inherited a natural dislike for spoilt food. No one ever has the idea to eat rotten and smelly meat and a butcher who sells rotten meat will be punished by law.

Only in the past century have we been confronted with a huge amount of new unknown dangers.

The negative effects from Hiroshima to Chernobyl, the chemical accidents from Seveso and Bhopal to the court cases regarding wood preservatives can be rationalized, however our reflexes and instincts can't adjust as quickly.

This inability to swiftly adjust our instinctive and emotional reactions to new dangers turns out to be a disadvantage for us. Timber preservatives which endanger our health and environment however are available in hardware and trade shops even though these products are causing disease and sometimes even death to children and adults.

Court Case in Germany regarding synthetic Timber / Wood products.

Intellectually we have analyzed and registered this information and we know that the production, use and disposal of these products are very harmful to our environment.

We are aware that by burning treated wood dioxins and other harmful substances are being released into the atmosphere and cause health and environmental problems. Nevertheless, unbelievable amounts of synthetic and chemical adhesives and preservatives are being used each year. The difference between toxic preservatives and rotten meat is that we have known modern chemical poisons only for a relatively short time and we have not yet upgraded our protective reflexes.

This might be one explanation of why synthetic chemicals are still part of wood production. However, it is not necessary to use preservatives, chipboard or plywood panels anywhere in the home. None of the hundreds of year old buildings have been chemically 'preserved'. How simple, timeless and beautiful was our granddad's way of building? The laminated products of the modern petrochemical industry and plywood manufacturers just can't compare with this.

The shark causes more fear than wood preservation methods.

Chapter Five - An excursion into the world of healthy building and living

- **The building site the size of a wooden cube**
- **A breathing filter**
- **Heat a family home with two cubic meters of firewood through winter**
- **Timber floors in your bathroom**
- **Everyone can build an ecologically sustainable home**
- **The secret of the dusty staircase**
- **Why hemp goes well with Timber / Wood**

"I am not going to move into a block of glass, stone or concrete." Those were the words Albert Einstein used when he opted for a wood home, which still stands in the town of Caputh, close to Berlin.

The building site - the size of a wooden cube

As a young high school student, I was convinced that the art of successfully attending school was to retain and deliver the bare minimum required to pass exams. After the test, all that had been crammed in was deleted straight away. For the pubescent mental and soul live attends to other more pressing life issues. It speaks for the pedagogical skills of a few teachers that I had learned to integrate some of the things they conveyed.

I still remember today how our science teacher, a lady professor, explained the wondrous and magnificent way we humans breathe: if you were to spread open the pipe and bubble system of our lungs, it would be very thin and cover an area about the size of a football field. On one side of this thin membrane the oxygen-poor blood flows while on the other side oxygen-rich air streams past. The blood absorbs oxygen through this thin surface membrane by a process called osmosis.

Equally simply, you can explain why wood is such a superior building material for a healthy and comfortable lifestyle. Similar to the human lung, wood has an incredibly fine cellular system, consisting of thin membranes and intercellular spaces. Cell membranes themselves are a system of pores and fine tubules. The result of this delicate texture is the same as in our lungs: an incredibly large 'internal surface area'.

Dr. Erwin Thoma

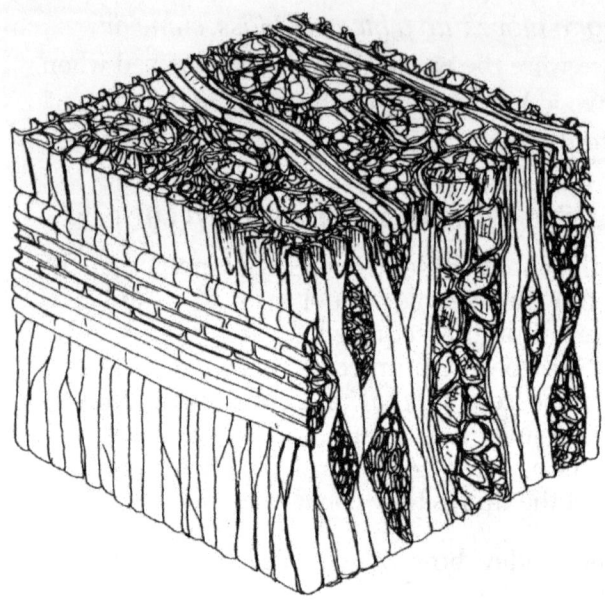

The internal surface area of wood.

One cubic centimeter of cellulose (percentage wise the most important ingredient of wood) has the unimaginable internal surface area of approximately six million square centimeters. In other words a game dice of cellulose has a surface area large enough (600 square meters) for a single family home, garden included. This fine structure has the effect of a sponge and acts like an air filter. Wood absorbs and filters harmful and smelly substances, retains and releases moisture and reduces electromagnetic smog inside the house.

Why do we perceive the atmosphere in an alpine cabin as particularly pleasant and cozy? Whereas our hair stands up when we enter a brand-new building with sealed and laminated floors, painted wall and ceiling panels. Wood connects with us via our senses of smell, touch, taste and vision. It provides us with a sense of strength, comfort and safety.

A fundamental requirement of healthy homes is that our buildings act as a third skin. This requirement is ingeniously and wonderfully fulfilled by wood. One thing we need to consider though: skin is supposed to breathe and must not be clogged or 'sealed' by airtight coatings, paints and glues. Otherwise, wood fares similarly to the lungs of a heavy smoker!

You will find more information about how you can treat wooden surfaces in a natural, low-maintenance way and retain your wood's ability to breath in a later part of this book. There are countless examples where you can see that natural surfaces are possible in low maintenance conditions.

A breathing filter

Because untreated wood is able to breathe, it lowers and harmonizes concentration levels of other substances suspended in the air, like gases, steam and odors and keeps all levels closer to what we experience as healthy, comfortable and beneficial.

A three-hour experiment showed how 0.4 m2 of untreated wooden cladding per m3 room volume absorbed Formaldehyde from the atmosphere. Without airing the room, the Formaldehyde levels were reduced from 1.2 ppm (equivalent to the smoke of 25 cigarettes) to 0.1 ppm. This result equals the reduction of 1/12 of the original concentration!

For wood to participate in a healthy gas exchange and moisture balancing act in your home, it needs to be untreated, uncoated, unclogged and preferably unglued.

Quoted: Bernhard Leisse: 'Holz natuerlich behandeln', Heidelberg 1994. 'Treating Wood Naturally', Heidelberg 1994.

Heat a family home with two cubic meters of firewood through winter

In the mid-1980s, the first trend towards solar energy was surfacing in Germany and Austria. Talks, literature, owner–builder groups, buying cooperatives and government funding were becoming more common and the first solar panels appeared in gardens and on roof tops. Depending on people's point-of-view, solar panels were either laughed at or praised.

Enthused by this idea, we installed some self-made panels[6] in our garden. When taking a shower or bath now, we enjoy the fact that the sun has warmed the water. Many years have passed and this solar installation has worked without a hitch and without any maintenance! Nowadays we are able to implement the use of solar even better than we did with our retro-fit.

Obviously one can save the most energy where you use the most; 90–95% of the energy usage of an average household in the state of 'Salzburg' is used for heating and hot water.

In 1993 Monika, Andreas and their son Daniel fulfilled their dream of an energy-efficient home and built a remarkable solid wood home in the 'Salzachtal'. Even during a long and hard alpine winter, the family uses only one to two cubic meters of fire wood instead of the usual 10 to 20 cubic meters. While they are warm and comfy, they also heat the domestic water supply at the same time. This family reduced their yearly energy consumption to a tenth of what they previously used and makes considerable savings.

Most of the energy used for heating is not created by burning firewood but by solar collectors on the roof and a

---

[6]*Austria is the pioneering country of solar energy. In 1994 there were already more than one million square meters of solar panels installed.*

large winter garden which stretches all along the south side of the home.[7] The extra cost for insulation and solar panels was absorbed by leaving out the usual bay windows and balconies which are so common in this area. The ideal orientation of the house towards the sun was at no extra cost and collecting river rocks to use as a heat sink (in one of the rooms in their cellar) was only a personal effort. On a sunny day, the hot air from the solar collector heats up the river rocks and on a cloudy or bad weather day, this heat sink releases warm air which is blown into the Hypokausten System of the house.

This simple recipe integrated their personal energy use with nature's cycles:

Insulation + solar panels + natural untreated wood + winter garden are more important than bay windows and balconies. None of the building materials contains synthetic glues or preservatives.

The result is impressive indeed:

From a cost point-of-view, this house was slightly more costly to build than the average house however the future benefits for health, maintenance and energy costs are substantial.

When I paid them a visit on a cold but sunny day in January, I saw smoke rising from every chimney in the area and smelt the burning wood in the air. However, their low-energy house didn't have any smoke rising from it at all. Monika was sitting in the winter garden with Daniel and the cat. Andreas was working in his warm office and the sun was shining 'free' of cost.

---

[7]*In the Northern Hemisphere, the sun is highest in the south and in the Southern Hemisphere it is highest in the north.*

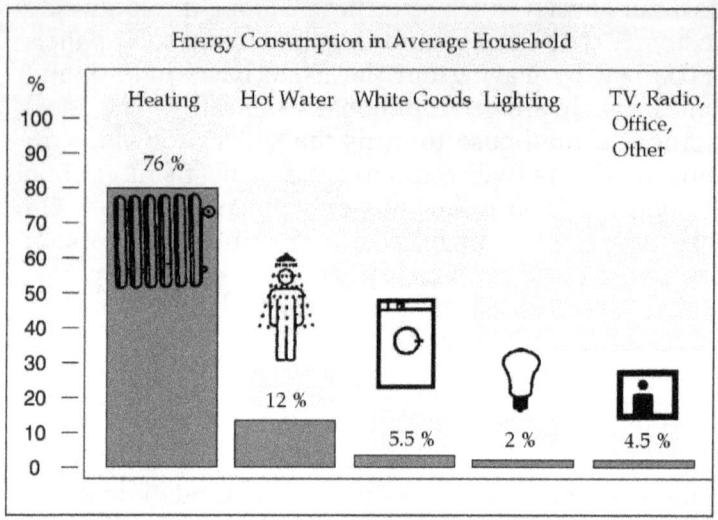

Graphic supplied by Energy and Environment Department of the Salzburger (Austrian) State Government.

'Holz 100' - the building solution

The realization of my dream to create the very best buildings in the world is the development of our prefabricated solid Holz 100 House. A good energy-efficient home should not only be comfortable, natural and healthy. It needs to have excellent ratings regarding insulation (heat, cold, acoustic, electromagnetic radiation), fire safety, and air conditioning.

We found wood has many hidden qualities and we developed a traditional building technique into a new and healthy 'High Tech' innovation. The name means pure, 100% wood, nothing added. With a Holz 100 house, walls, ceilings and roof are made of large, solid and prefabricated wooden panels which can be erected in a very short space of time. These elements are made of untreated wood, no glues, laminates, or nails. To build with Holz 100 elements results in high-performance ratings which previously were thought of as impossible.

Holz 100 elements consist of boards and battens which, piece by piece, are lying horizontally next to each other making up the size of the panel. The second layer is stacked diagonally, the third layer vertically and so on. These layers form elements as thick as is required for walls, ceilings and floors.

The question now is how to keep them together and end up with cohesive building elements. The solution lies in wood itself.

When I was young, I was trained to be an explosives expert and became quite fascinated by explosives. Holding a stick of dynamite in my hand and knowing the hidden power it had, made me shudder. I was unaware then, that a wooden dowel about the same size would be able to split mighty rocks.

As early as antiquity itself and at the time of ancient Egypt, large blocks of rock were exploded and split by swelling wood. Lacking explosives and machinery, people fitted bone-dry wooden dowels into holes and cracks. Then, they just added water. Dry wood absorbs the moisture and expands. This irresistibly strong force even splits granite boulders. It is one of the strongest forces in nature and we harness it for our Holz 100 elements.

Holes are drilled through all the element's layers, each consisting of individual battens lying next to each other. Then kiln-dried wooden dowels are driven into the neatly fitting holes. Even in dry climates a wooden wall always retains rest moisture (ranging from 6% to 15% relative moisture content). The moisture of the surrounding wood is absorbed by the dowel which swells and expands tightly into its hole. Because no room climate anywhere in the world can be as dry as in a kiln, this joint can't ever be dissolved other than by drilling it out.

Holz 100 - wall element

Because the layers are stacked crisscross, the Holz 100 element is solid. It can be rendered, tiled or painted. The advantages of building with purely natural, untreated wood are mainly in the following areas:

1. Fire safety
2. Warmth and noise insulation
3. Air conditioning
4. Cooling down time
5. Radiation shielding
6. Earthquake safety.

To stay within the framework of this book, I have only mentioned some short and simple descriptions for the layperson. Scientific tests, publications and building certifications were undertaken at several different universities and institutes in Austria, Germany, Norway, Japan and the USA and are available through the Erwin Thoma Research Centre.

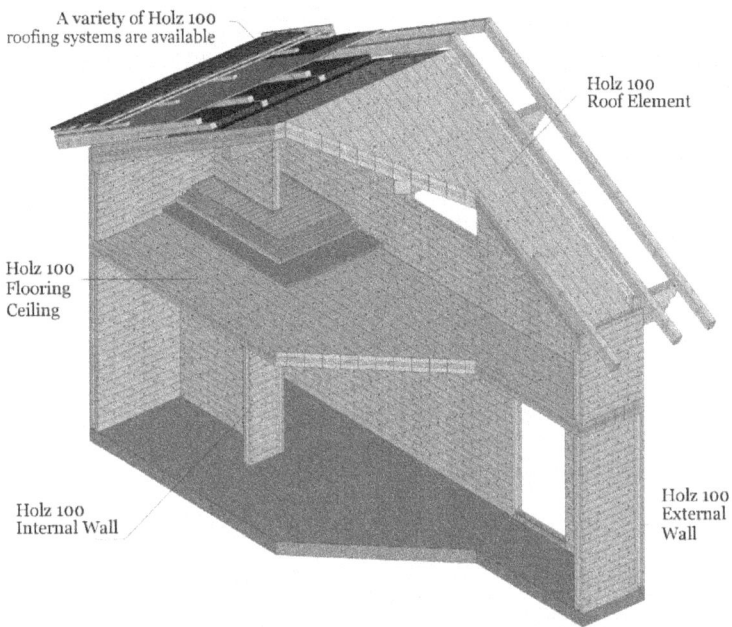

1. Fire safety rating

The European standard in high-tech woodblock and frame buildings (with normal, average wall, ceiling and roof thicknesses) is maximal F 30. This means that the building element resists a flame at 1000 degrees Celsius for 30 minutes. Holz 100 elements reached top ratings of up to F 180! This means six times safer than the usual reinforced concrete or brick walls offer. The ceiling ratings are even better.

Why? Wood burns well when it is thin and in contact with plenty of air. However, a thick block of wood hardly burns at all. It chars fairly slowly, approximately 0.5–0.7 mm per minute. In a Holz 100 House, every ceiling, wall and floor is a thick, fire-resistant block of wood.

While flame testing reinforced concrete walls, the cold side of the wall (which was not directly exposed to the flame) was showing in some areas a +400 degrees Celsius temperature rise after only 30 minutes. This happens because the reinforcement iron inside the concrete turns glowing hot and conducts the heat rapidly throughout the whole wall element.

While flame-testing a Holz 100 wall element, the hottest spot on the cold side after 90 minutes was maximal only +1.8 degrees Celsius higher than the temperature taken at the start of the test. Wood is a warmth shield and even after hours of external flame testing and heat, its innermost is quite unchanged. This is incredibly important for safety reasons, particularly in large buildings. Many fires expand faster via heat than flames. Even if this sounds incredible, wood is safer than concrete.

2. Thermal insulation

The inside of a Holz 100 element consists of layers of roughly sawn battens pressed together. This creates microscopic thin layers of air which is not circulating and results in excellent additional insulating properties. After recognizing this effect, we increased the ratings by cutting more fine grooves into the battens surface. The results were a world record in thermal insulation!

Compared with all the structural building methods, Holz100 is the building material with the very best natural thermal insulation.

Consider the following: To achieve a thermal insulation rating of 0.3 Wm2K, which is the current European norm aspired to, an architect who wanted to build without insulation, would have to use the following wall thicknesses for his buildings:

- Reinforced concrete: 726cm
- Average brick: 60 cm
- Conventional Timber and Glue-lam wood products: 47 cm
- Holz 100: 27 cm

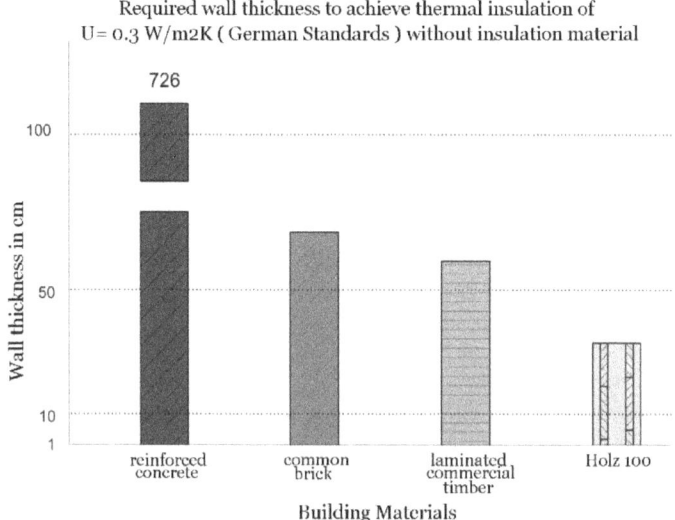

3. Acclimatizing and cooling down time

The time it takes for a house to heat up in summer and cool down in winter depends on the insulation materials used. A bigger influence though comes from the building material itself. At the University of Graz, we tested three commonly used building systems.

The experiment was simple:

A wood frame wall, a brick wall and a Holz 100 wall were prepared with insulation materials to achieve the same thermal insulation rating. Each wall was exposed to a constant temperature of 21degrees Celsius.

To simulate winter in the laboratory, the outside temperature was then lowered to minus 10 degrees Celsius and the inside heating turned off, as if the tenants turned off the heating and left. We applied the same conditions to all three walls and measured the time it took the cold to penetrate through the wall and reach zero degrees on the internal wall surface.

Here are the results:

- The wood frame wall was insulated with mineral wool and took 41 hours

- The brick wall insulated with polystyrene took 259 hours

- The 'Holz 100' wall was insulated with hemp cooled down after 777 hours

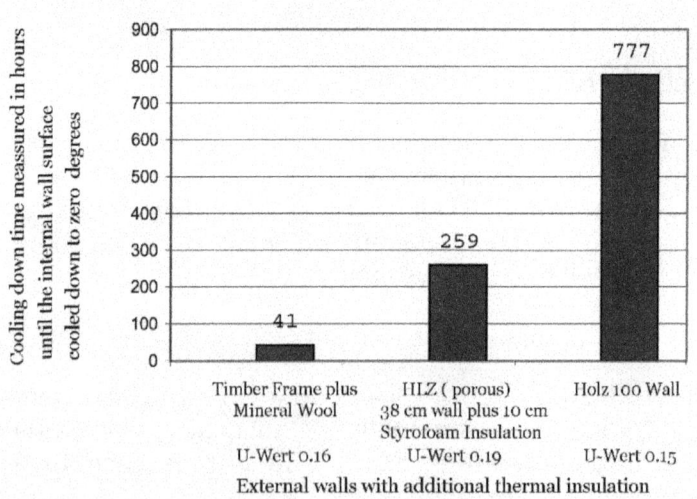

Cooling Down Time

Wood also acclimatizes a building more efficiently. Not only in winter when it acts as a heat conductor but during summer too. It is thermally slow and more effective than any other building material. This led us to build more and more roofs with solid wood panels in warmer areas which achieved much better ratings than with roof trusses, because they acted like wood frame walls.

I remember a quote by Rudolf Steiner (German/Austrian, founder of Waldorf Schools and Biodynamic Agriculture): "It is the mass of the building which creates a good atmosphere. I would add: "The best way to create a good quality atmosphere indoors is by building with natural wood."

4. Radiation shielding

While building one of our first Holz 100 homes, I noticed that the mobile phone reception was very weak inside the newly erected building and I decided to investigate this phenomenon further.

The Munich University of the Federal Armed Forces became our scientific research partner and conducted more than 700 laboratory tests. Practically all of the well-known building systems on the market were tested for their protective qualities regarding electromagnetic radiation. The results were surprising even to their radiation experts and technicians.

Natural wood as we use in Holz 100 achieved the best results. Holz 100 panels blocked high frequency mobile phone radiation better than reinforced concrete, bricks or other commonly used prefabricated building systems. The complete scientific publication about this issue can be viewed through the Erwin Thoma Scientific Research Center.

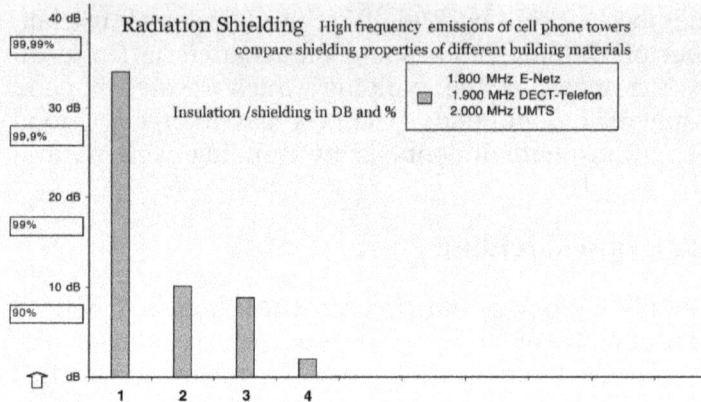

From: 'Reducing the amount of high frequency radiation penetrating buildings', May 2000 updated in 02/02 by Prof. Peter Pauli and Dr. Dietrich Moldan.

1. THOMA Holz 100, consisting of 2.4 cm Larch rough sawn exterior wall /37 cm Spruce / 4 cm interior Larch (for fire safety)

2. Concrete 16 cm with reinforcement (2.400 kg/m3)

3. Vertical coring brick 36 cm (800 kg/m3), render on one side

4. Prefabricated House, wall 0.9 cm KH-Render / 4 EPS / 1.3 Particleboard/14 Mineral wool / 1.8 GKP

5. "Reduction of High Frequency Radiation penetration in Buildings", May 2000, updated in 02/02, by Prof. Peter Pauli und Dr. Dietrich Moldan.

Cell phones of the first generation often didn't work in Holz 100 buildings. Meanwhile the small percentage of rest radiation which enters through the window frames is enough for it to work.

The tenant of a Holz 100 home still has the advantage that the radiation density is drastically lower inside the building compared to the outside. Laboratory tests showed that Holz 100 elements blocked up to 99% radiation, depending on frequency.

5. Acoustic insulation

For a long time, people thought a wood house, though comfortable and romantic, was just not very soundproof. Holz 100 houses consist of 100% wooden elements which have excellent sound attenuation.

An architect challenged me with the following task: Can you build a hotel with Holz 100 that would have the best-sound proofed rooms anywhere?

And we built the 'quietest wood hotel in the world' with Holz 100 for the Auer Family in the Tyrolean 'Oetztal'. Every room of this hotel has an acoustic rating twice as good as the building norms and regulations for hotels prescribe. Please note, the building standards for hotels are very strict and some hotels cannot even comply.

To those people which still have concerns about the Holz 100 ratings, I suggest spending a wellness weekend in the 'Hotel Waldklause' in the Austrian 'Oetztal'. This saves long discussions and so far has convinced everyone who doubted the superiority of wood.

6. Earthquake safety

Because this book is not meant to be scientifically dry, I will outline some examples which make common sense instead of presenting trial reports and numbers.

You find the oldest wooden buildings on earth in Japan, a region which is well-known for its earthquakes and its instability. Temples and pagodas up to six stories high were built without glues or metals and have survived the worst earthquakes for the past 1600 years! Holz 100 is using the same principle and it is not surprising that Holz 100 homes easily fulfill the Japanese earthquake building standards, the tightest and strictest in the world. As a matter of fact, this book's first translation was for the technology enthusiastic Japanese market. By now, there are many Holz 100 buildings in Japan which have survived several earthquakes intact; one of them rating 8 on the Richter scale.

Holz 100 is a method which brings together old traditional knowledge and modern technology. It provides protection and safety for people living in Holz 100 houses. When this book was first published 12 years ago, the idea to build the best ecological house using untreated wood was looked down on as a sort of eco joke. Today, there are Holz 100 Manufacturers in Austria, Germany, Norway and preparations for manufacturers in the United States and other countries.

By now, many then-unimaginable buildings have been built with untreated and natural wood including more than 1000 homes, large hotels in Italy, Austria and Norway, health clinics, hospitals, schools and childcare centers, the University for Forestry and Timber in Oslo, and sacred buildings like a church in Japan. Working in tune with nature results in building the best houses where people feel comforted, safe and stay healthy for many years to come. [8]

The master carpenter, bathrooms and wooden floors

Who isn't familiar with a hoarse throat in winter, when the central heating is running on full steam? The dry air stirred dust strain our breathing and can be as unpleasant as very high humidity. A superior building material buffers and balances moisture independent of whether it is extremely humid or dry. Untreated wood has a large inner surface

---

[8] *You will find more Information for this system on the internet: www.thoma.at or contact the Erwin Thoma Research Centre for Natural Timber Processing, Hasling35, A - 5622, Goldegg Tel: (0043) 0 6415/8910.*

area where the many pores, capillaries and micro-tubules react to changes in moisture levels of the surrounding.

While the humidity rises, wood absorbs moisture and dries up the air. When humidity levels drop and the air dries up, wood releases some of the retained moisture back into the atmosphere and keeps a nice balance. Timber in a building is the ideal moisture buffer. The more natural wood there is in a house, the better the buffer effect.

Whoever still has concerns about untreated wood being suitable for bathrooms will be surprised by the following. It is true, bathrooms have the most extreme climatic changes in any home and in the early years of manufacturing, I too declined to build bathroom floors. I was afraid the spaces between the floorboards would end up being too big and the movement of the wood too much.

However the following experience led me to a vital realization:

One day a colleague carpenter ordered a cherry tree floor for one of his clients and didn't tell me what room the floor was meant to go in. As promised, we delivered his cherry tree floorboards and a little while later, he rang to let me know that the floor turned out very nicely. I asked him if his clients were happy with it and he said: "very much so!"

A few months later, I went to visit him and was greatly surprised to find out he was the client. He led me into his bathroom and showed me his cherry tree floor, very neat and tight. No sign of gaps and movement between the boards. The carpenter told me with a grin on his face that he knew about my cautiousness and he wanted to spare me sleepless nights. But he always knew, that one could use untreated wood even in bathrooms, as long as it has been harvested at the right time.

The result of the bathroom floor inspection were three happy faces: his wife's, looking proudly at her beautiful natural cherry floor, the joyful carpenter's and my own face which must have looked rather surprised, judging by his chuckling. Since this event, we have delivered and installed many natural wooden floors for bathrooms and found here too, natural and untreated wood balances the air humidity.

For example: if the humidity in a room rises from 35% to 65%, 1m2 of spruce cladding absorbs up to 10 grams of moisture in 12 hours and dries up the air. This works the opposite way too. If the air in a room is suddenly very dry, wood slowly releases moisture back into the air.

We found, and you too can try the following experiment, that after installing natural wood ceilings, wall claddings and/or floors, the mirror rarely fogs over and hardly any condensation water appears when you have a shower.

You need to be aware though, plywood and chipboard, wood component panels sealed and laminated surfaces totally negate the buffer effect of wood. You only get these advantages when you use solid, untreated, adhesive-free wood which is able to breathe freely.

The eternally dusty stairway

Think about the crackle when you pull a synthetic jumper over your head. Synthetic carpets are getting charged just by walking on them. The famous zap when holding the door knob is the corresponding discharge. Electrostatic charge is caused by dry and heated air (central heating) moving past nonconductive synthetic surfaces. The resulting load is larger if the surfaces are less conductive. You rarely experience this with natural materials like pure wool or linen.

Building Biologists[9] ensure that there are as few electrostatic chargeable surfaces as possible in living areas.

---

[9]*Wikipedia definition: Building Biology (or Baubiologie as it was coined in Germany) is a field of building science investigating the indoor living environment for a variety of irritants. Practitioners believe the environment of residential, commercial and public*

The human body in itself naturally has a weak electric shield surrounding it. This weak electric field repels dust, dirt particles and bacteria etc. Rooms with a strong electromagnetic charge disturb this natural protective field and sensitive people can experience allergies, inflamed mucus membranes, colds, headaches etc. In Europe this is called the 'sick building syndrome'.

Another disadvantage of statically charged surfaces is the tendency to attract dust and dirt, like the surfaces of TV screens or stereos attract lots of dust. This problem is easy to solve. Just make sure you have as much natural and untreated wood in your home as possible. If you want to treat wooden surfaces, use only natural bees wax or resins.

Floors, walls and ceilings made of untreated wood will not affect the natural occurring electromagnetic fields in your home negatively. This characteristic is one of the reasons an old alpine cabin feels so much more comfortable than an apartment with painted surfaces.

Here is a short story by a young couple in our neighborhood. A couple of years ago they experienced an interesting phenomenon in an unexpected way. When their home was built, the contractor installed a floor made of Ash in the entry area of their house. The surface of this floor was then treated with natural resin and bees wax. The stair case in the foyer connected the rest of the house with the entry area and was built by another carpenter who lacquered the stairs with a commercial water based product.

"Horrible", the wife complained. These stairs act like a dust magnet, it seems they attract all the dust from the whole house. The waxed and oiled floors in the other rooms do

buildings can affect the health of the occupants, producing a restful or stressful environment. Important areas of building biology building materials and processes, electromagnetic fields (EMFs) and radiation (EMR) and indoor air quality (IAQ).

not, just the stair case was forever covered in a layer of dust. The wife would mop it three times a day and complain about it many times. Her husband finally promised to take off the varnish and oil it as he had done it with the other floors. There was no doubt that she would insist on him doing what he promised to do.

What is more hygienic?

An American study[10] into salmonellas and kitchen cutting boards showed drastic results. Salmonellas actually die after a few minutes on a natural, untreated woodcutting board. Whereas plastic cutting boards have salmonella thrive and increase in population. Think about laminated kitchen counters and cutting boards which many people think are more hygienic than untreated wood.

What emits radiation in a home?

This is not about the sun radiation or the smile on a happy persons face. It is about comparing all types of radiation which one is exposed to in living situations due to the building materials which have been used.

The average exposure to radioactive radiation[11] through naturally occurring and man sources:

The average radiation burden in Germany is 150 millirem (mr). Just by living in homes with a variety of building materials, the following has to be added:

- Granite/Slag: +150 mr = total 300 mr
- Plaster: +65 mr = total 215 mr
- Brick and Concrete: +20 mr = total 170 mr

---

[10]Study into "Plastic and Wooden Cutting Boards" by Dean Oliver, Ph.D.

[11] Guidelines by the Bavarian Society of Nuclear Medicine.

- Natural Wood: -10 mr = total 140 mr

The only building material which can actually lower radiation is natural wood.

Chapter Six - Our forests are our best bet

- **Alternatives to fossil fuels**
- **Waste - an unknown word**
- **Fossil fuels and throwaway society**
- **Forests sustain us with energy and clean air**
- **The forests' closed energy circuit**

Technology and science has brought us many discoveries, advances and life changing events which our ancestors wouldn't have been able to imagine. Nevertheless, our basic life conditions depend on the preservation of countless ingenious, small and large natural cycles, one of which is the "Tree –Wood –Mulch/Ash–Tree...." cycle.

If we want a healthy and happy life style for our children and grandchildren on this planet, this is one example where we need to change our perception and attitude.

Alternatives to fossil fuels

In the 21st century we are very lucky to have limitless mobility. We spend hours every day to get to and from work and travel from one continent to another for relaxation. We transport potatoes hundreds of miles all through Europe just to get them washed and returned and then processed somewhere else. Tree trunks are being shipped from Russia to Germany and Austria as well as from central Europe to Japan to be manufactured into particle boards.

Statistics show the increase in exhaust fumes, traffic accidents and land use for more road infrastructure. But does higher mobility really equate to a better quality of life? Restructuring local supply sources means much more than just reducing exhaust fumes.

While I am writing this, I remember a high school trip. We made a raft of round tree trunks and for days we travelled down the Danube River through all of Austria. I still carry these impressions and memories within me and I will never forget the landscapes.

When I look at our winter garden I remember the trees which I selected and where they had grown in our local forest. I remember the Ash, Spruce and Oaks I used for the floors in our home. I also am thinking about the local farmer who fills our Swiss Pine chest with fresh and organic grain, or the milk and butter which is from our neighbor and is not trucked through several countries. My wife makes our yogurt and even the linen we use for clothing comes from our local hemp farmers.

I realize that this is not necessarily possible for everyone, however, with a little more thought we could do much better with the world's resources.

Waste - an unknown word

The best teacher I could ever have wished for was our granddad who was a carpenter well into his nineties. When he returned back home after the war with Russia, he had a short recovery period and then went back to his much loved vocation carpentry.

With simple means he built a home for his family with wood which had been locally harvested at the right time. He built everything himself, right down to the windows and chairs. The comfort and soul of this small cottage still enchants us each time we visit 'Urliopa' (granddad) with our children.

The stories he tells are rich in experience and have our ears ringing with excitement. Here are some bits I would like to share with you.

Today, 50 years after our granddad built and furnished his home, the energy which is needed to build a home of the same size (depending on the kind of materials) is up to 130 times more.

High energy consumption is an indicator of abnormal development:[12]

---

[12]*Environment and Energy Consultants of the State Government Salzburg 1995*

A Future with Natural Wood

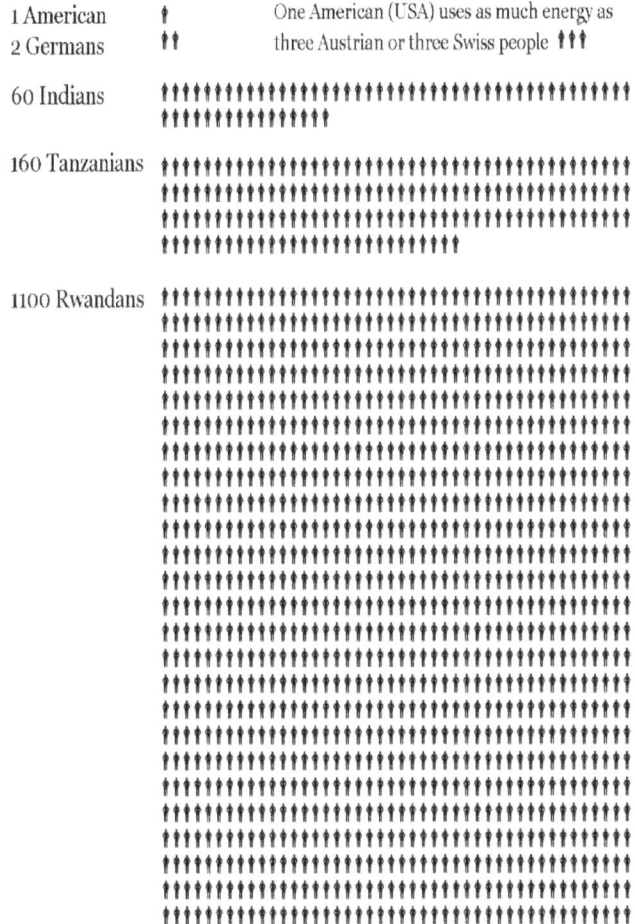

The curious thing of this comparison is that modern buildings are not necessarily nicer, healthier or more durable. Actually the contrary often is the case.

In Granddad's home you feel comfortable with a sense of warmth and wellbeing. There is no dampness or mold growing; the air is free of formaldehyde and dioxins because no particle board, plastic windows or synthetic carpets/ underlay have been used. All of which are very common in most modern buildings.

He worked at a time, where it was normal to source as much as possible locally. This was not only the case for building materials, but also clothes, food and many other things.

Before presenting the argument that people were very poor, we should look at traditional life styles and adapt what can be useful to us today. The words rubbish, scrap and junk were nonexistent for our ancestors. Everything was reused and found another purpose. Building a rubbish dump for the town? Granddad just shook his head, back then nobody had heard of anything like that.

He told us that they always wore shirts made from hand-woven linen. It was a natural fiber and allowed the skin to breath, even on the hottest days. A ripped shirt wasn't ready for the bin; it would be mended several times before the faithful garment was used as a cleaning cloth for many years to come. When these rags began to disintegrate they still weren't considered rubbish but detoured via the compost back to the fields where they originally came from. Effectively, the compost was helping to grow more linen shirts.

Granddad contributes his strong health to his simple but quality life style. He never had slipped disks or back pain, even though the work back then was physically harder than it is now. His attitude is not really antiquated but does represent the "ultimate green" living standard. Just imagine what we could gain by taking advantage of his experience.

Fossil fuels and throwaway society

Honestly, who hasn't been blinded by the seemingly endless shopping opportunities of our affluent consumer society? We love to refurbish even when not necessary. We buy new furniture, appliances and electronics and discard the old items. But where does the "old" stuff end up?

My childhood in the sixties was very much shaped by the endless trust in technology and science. Since then Laboratories constantly develop new molecular structures and materials which have previously not existed on earth. Manufacturers mass produce goods in huge quantities, giving us a feeling of consumer freedom which would not be possible with traditional and natural materials like wood, stone and plant fibers.

Huge advertising efforts are made to replace natural materials and methods with synthetics, adhesives and cocktails of a diverse variety of inscrutable chemical combinations. These new materials are mostly produced from mineral oil. Synthetic fabrics, paints, laminates, foams, plastics......the list of oil products is endless. Similarly long is the list of harmful by - and waste products, which are part of the long process from mining to the finished product and its disposal in landfill.

Even wood is not really wood anymore. Just look closely at plywood and other laminated boards and you find it is a mixture of wood shavings or chips mixed with toxic glues and paints. It takes decades before we find out how humans, animals and plant life react to these materials. Resulting health issues like allergies, asthma and damage to our genes are only part of the world our children grow into. Toxic waste dumps here and in third world countries where our waste ends up, cause even more harm. A disposable society which creates this amount of garbage is most likely to lose interest and joy in work and life.

And yes, we are hearing the wakeup call now. News of lethal accidents like the catastrophe of Bhopal, Exxon Valdez, Three Mile Island, Chernobyl, Fukushima... have rocked the trust in scientific and technical progress. Climate change, mega traffic congestions, diseases and allergies which were unknown to our grandparent's generation are showing us the limits of progress today.

Now we have a great opportunity and the task to refocus on a lifestyle which will serve man and nature. In the end, we will be proud and fulfilled with our work.

While writing this, I am sitting on an old but very comfortable chair that our granddad built with his simple hand tools. The furniture he created is still adding value to us and his great grandchildren. I look at the hardwood floors and know that these floors are going to be walked on by future generations. Craftsmanship and natural materials produce lasting products which give more and longer enjoyment than synthetic consumer articles can ever do. Lasting quality is the true measure of the green movement.

I hope we all find lifelong enjoyment and the careful and enthusiastic handling of precious materials which nature presents us with is the first step in this direction.

Often it is the old and wise people which help us open our eyes to new worlds. I experienced this for the first time when I was practicing on the wooden stilts my granddad built for me. I remember our old neighbor who always was there with a helping hand; particularly at those difficult times after our dad died a much too early death. I am thinking about the old forester Fritz Leoffler, who shared the secrets of the 'Karwendel Mountains' with me, when I was a young forester. I think about my grandma, who always stood behind my wife and me and encouraged us to stay on the path we had chosen when we were a young couple. She also taught us to not take ourselves too seriously. Having been happily married for 60 years, she certainly was a great role model.

We are blessed to watch how our children's love for their Oma and Opa blossoming. When "Brucker Nonna" tells a story gesticulating hands and feet, none of the grandchildren ever gets the idea to turn on the TV. - "Our Nonna is brilliant!" Enjoying these treasures in our everyday life fulfills us and we do not need shopping therapy to make us feel better.

Energy Cycles

By Franz Gillinger

We turn our back towards the sun
And mine coal in the mountains.
We turn our back towards the sun
And drill for oil.
We turn our backs toward the sun
And split atoms.
When will we turn around?

Nature is reaching out, let's take her hand. We can observe natural energy cycles where one day's energy production contains a multiple of what we spend in a whole year. Solar energy used straight from the collectors could cover about 70-80% of our residential energy demand for hot water and heating. With energy produced from wood, hydro and wind power we could cover a large part of our total energy demand in the medium and long run. Despite of this, the European energy supply still consists of approximately 75% of non-renewable energy like mineral oil, gas, coal.

Planet earth became habitable millions of years ago when carbon from the atmosphere was being absorbed and stored in forests and turned into coal, oil and gas. The way we use fossil fuels today reverses this process and if we don't change, this direction will lead us to an inhospitable planet earth.

Every day nature re grows millions of cubic meters of wood in the forests of our planet. Just in tiny Austria itself, every second grows one cubic meter of wood. A cubic meter is a cube which is one meter long, high and deep purely made of wood.

Every day the sun evaporates unimaginable amounts of water from the oceans into the atmosphere. This water returns as rain and fills creeks, lakes and rivers which lead it back to the oceans. The suns power also causes air movements. Winds and storms could run all the machinery of this world. And the sun rises every day, what more could we want?

In Austria alone, one cubic meter of wood grows in one second!

What does it take for us to realize that our energy demand is tiny compared to these powerful natural processes. When will we recognize that nature's designs are the most economic and wholesome?

Once we understand how to tune into that huge natural energy current, we won't need to waste fossil fuels like oil, gas, coal and nuclear energy and nature can reestablish the natural balance of our earth.

By the time trees have grown from a seedling to a gigantic old tree and broken down, they have had decades of working out rankings with each other to establish their social position in the forest hierarchy. Animals and the whole forest community has been protected and nourished by them. The trees also provide for their own existence by supplying leaves and pine needles to the forest floor to produce enough mulch for the coming generations. Finally when the tree has fulfilled its need for procreation it leaves the same way as it came. Old tree giants collapse, break down and enrich the soil with nutrients for the next generation in which they live on.

This process from tree to mulch is in perfect natural order and a very productive cycle. The suns energy and the Co_2 which is absorbed by the tree is released back into the atmosphere, when the tree is rotting.

I wish for an avalanche of solar and low energy homes, of wood, hemp and many uses of natural materials for our future generations. Mothers buying toys and fathers building homes set this trend and their demands will reach the people responsible in the economic and politic echelons.

Let's make the most of this sacred cycle and live in harmony with nature. Conservation means appreciate and manage our forests appropriately in a loving and caring way.

Forests sustain us with energy and clean air

As mentioned, the European energy supply relies on approximately 75 percent from non-renewable sources like oil, gas and coal and this has a decisive disadvantage: it threatens our environment and our health!

Burning one ton of oil releases 2.8 tons of Co_2 waste into the air. This means the intense use of oil, gas and coal causes the rise of Co_2 into the atmosphere and relates to all the associated risks as warming of the atmosphere.

The question is: does our modern consumer society cause these results and if so, do we have to put up with it? What are useful alternatives?

Our forests can be part of our energy supply. The forest takes Co_2 from the air and uses it as a building block to grow trees. If we build products which have a long lifecycle like furniture or homes, Co2 stays bound in the form of 250 kilogram carbon per cubic meter wood. A family which decides to build a wood home takes about 20 000 kilogram carbon from the air.

A tree is the largest, self-renewable storage sink of CO_2 and sun energy. It is a power plant which produces oxygen and clean air for us humans. When burned correctly, wood releases not one gram more Co2 than it had absorbed from the atmosphere during its growth. A perfectly balanced and closed circuit which is not compromising the Co2 balance sheet of our environment.

Best Practice: To utilize wood best and reduce pollution, use only dry and well-seasoned wood. It should be stacked neatly off the ground, protected from rain, and have dried for at least 6 months. Wood burns best when the moisture content is around 20 %.

When lighting a fire, keep the air supply open and flames intense. Dark dense smoke contains gases which were not burned and is an indicator that the combustion is not good enough. Maintain and clean the wood stove and flue once a year because soot does not conduct heat and reduces the efficiency. Wood from conifers has more resin and produces more soot. Hardwoods burn hotter; produce more heat and burn longer than softwoods. Always have more than one log on the fire, this gives the flames more surface and creates airflow to keep the fire going. To maintain airflow, empty the ashes regularly.

If we keep burning oil, gas or coal, we effectively release stored sun energy, because they too are of plant and organic matter. However the important difference is the toxic emissions like sulfur and nitrogen molecules which are being released by burning fossil fuels. Additionally, fossil fuels were created in millions of years whereas trees grow in decades or centuries.

If we use energy which has been stored for millions of earth years in a fraction of an earth second, we set something in motion which is out of our control, like the sorcerer's apprentice.

The ozone hole in our earth's atmosphere, our global climate changes and mass dying of trees are results of speeding up this slow cycle.

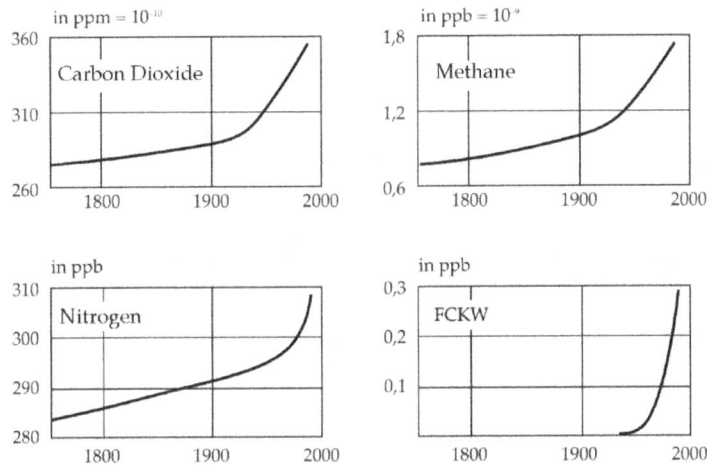

Greenhouse gases are mainly carbon monoxide, methane, nitrogen and FCKW. They prevent the radiation of heat from the earth into space and thus contribute to the rising temperatures on earth. The measured concentration of these gasses (apart from FCKW which has only been introduced in the last few decades) has risen constantly since 1800.

Source: Organization of World Meteorology. Measured in ppm = 10-6m, ppb= 10-9

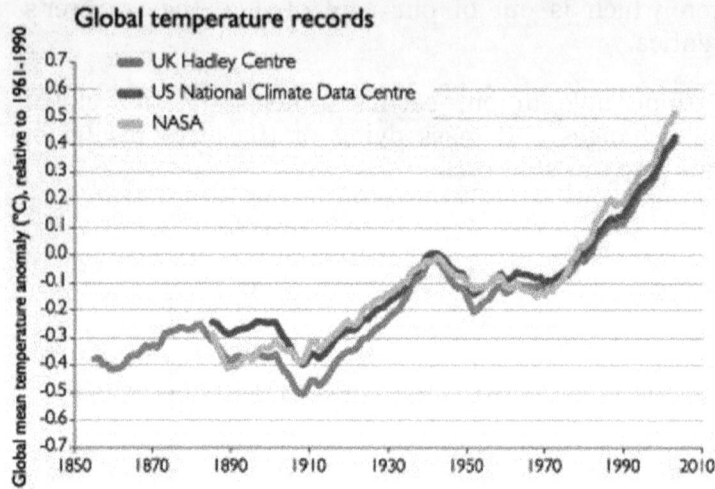

The three most complete global temperature records available – from the UK Hadley Centre, NASA, and the US National Climate Data Centre – all show a clear upward trend in global average temperatures over the last 150 years (calculated using an 11 year running average).

Science still is unable to identify the exact causes and prospects of the anticipated climate changes on earth and this causes endless political and environmental debates. There is no doubt that globally the average temperature has risen since 1880. If we keep wasting oil, gas and coal and continue plundering our planet, the whole/hole in the ozone layer will be of secondary importance.

We can best avoid environmental and climatic damage if we tune into natural energy cycles. We finally need to recognize the options nature presents us in form of renewable resources and learn how to use wood in ways which will allow us to safely recycle it after we have used it as furniture or building timber.

Maybe sit back for a moment and remember the last time you went for a walk through the forest. Can you feel the soft ground under your feet, the cool, fresh, spicy and healthy air? Don't you think the air freshening, solar power generating wood producing forest is a divine gift? It serves us daily free of charge and without fail. There is not one day where nature doesn't work for us.

We need to fulfill just one important criterion to keep this wonderful system running: treat wood only with natural products, so it can be released back into nature's cycle and decompose. In other words, avoid using chemical treatments, paints and adhesives. They are of manmade substances and turn wood into toxic waste which is not biodegradable when composted or released into the air and waterways.

The example of our middle European countries shows that all building materials and energy required for our daily life could be covered from sources which are harmless to our environment[13]. Every architect and builder could save an incredible amount of energy which is now being wasted. For example the choice of a wooden window means that only a 126th part of the energy is used compared to an aluminum window. Or the other way around, you could use the same energy which is being used to install one house with aluminum windows to fit 126 houses with wooden windows!

Compare the energy usage to produce windows, doors, floors, building, furniture etc.

---

[13] *'Der Sanfte Weg' – 'The Gentle Way', by Hans Kronberger und Hans Nagler, Uranus Verlag, Vienna.*

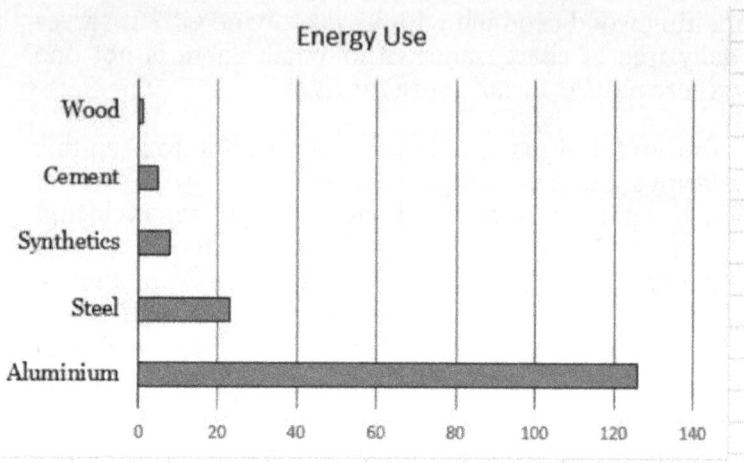

The energy used to produce 1 aluminum window could produce 126 Timber / Wood windows.

Sources:

Bavarian State Forestry Commission, Technical University Munich; Bavarian Advisory Committee for Forestry and Timber Management; Bavarian Ministry for Agriculture and Forestry; Federal Environment Ministry, Bonn.

This comparison can be applied to all types of building materials. Think about flooring (wood or synthetics), insulation (hemp or foam), doors, stairways, furniture and much more. Once we use this vast energy resource, our "solar powered generator forest" more effectively, we need less power plants, storage, transport and infrastructure. Our forests are the most energy rich resource available to us and we need to treat and manage nature's gift in a useful and sensible manner.

Here in Austria, if we were to use wood as building material for our homes (from the floor to the roof, furniture, heating, thermal power stations, to make paper) we still couldn't use up the yearly re growth of wood. There still would be enough trees left to decay and mulch the forest floor. According to statistics of the forestry inventory, only half of the combined yearly re growth from Germany and Austria together is being harvested. Most of it is being used in a wasteful and toxic way.

The use of toxic wood preservatives, paints and glues has turned modern wood products into toxic waste which cannot be returned to nature and close this wood cycle.

When we recognize this ingenious and simple resource and integrate our ways into the natural cycle, we will be able to fully replace fossil fuels with renewable energy.

Two villages are firing up

The saying goes: "The farmer won't eat what he doesn't know!"

In the local inn of the small village 'Bramberg' in 'Salzburger Land', discussions were running hot about a proposed project they called: 'Hackschnitzelheizung'.

"They want to build a heating plant for our village? One which burns wood chips? That must be a joke! It wouldn't work, impossible!"

"Maybe we should try it out?"

Isn't it crazy to heat our buildings with fossil fuels from afar, which have been mined and transported around the whole world and at the same time, our local woodchips and wood waste is being trucked to far away countries. It's not surprising that people living in the valleys are complaining about the amount of trucks on the roads.

The biomass power station in 'Bramberg' has now been running for many years and the unthinkable became reality. This small power station is able to supply the whole village with warmth. The emissions sank to less than those generated by just one family home with a badly adjusted oil heater.

Even just a generation ago, this was unthinkable. Today it is possible thanks to the advancements made in the heating and combustion technology.

Environmental impact study, emissions from central heating plants in kg/TJ

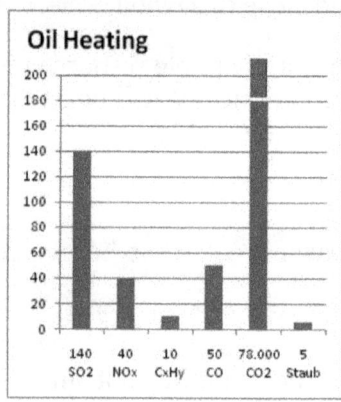

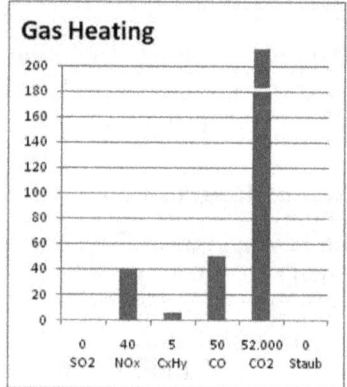

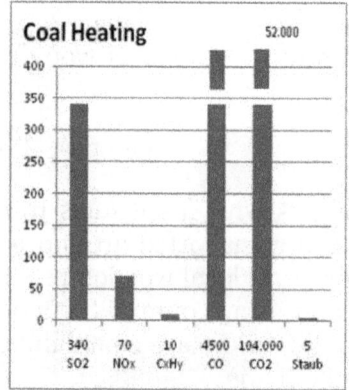

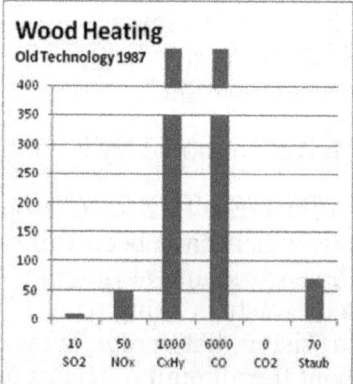

Energy report 1990 of the Austrian Government

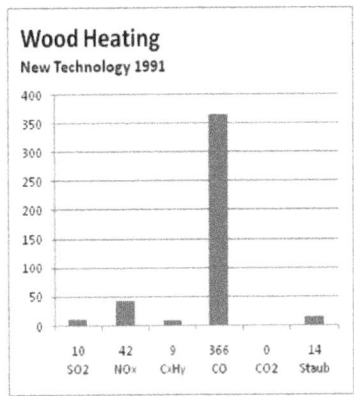 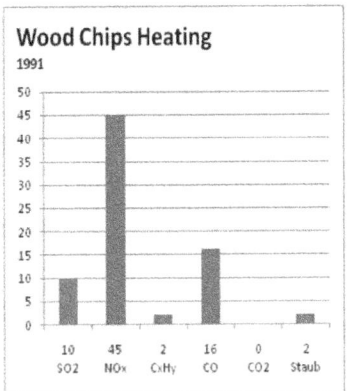

Department of Agricultural Technology, Wieselburg, Austria

The warmth which is generated by a centralized biomass power station is nothing else than sun energy stored in growing tress and closes a natural cycle. The technical advancements of biomass combustion are not only available to a few privileged communities. It has reached a stage now, where it is possible to build very small units that generate sufficient energy for single family homes. These small furnaces include an automatic stoker and ash removal. Generic versions are available in sizes suitable for single households up to large plants. Heating with renewable biomass at the push of a button is no utopian dream anymore.

The 'Bramberg' village centralized biomass power station is accommodated in a wooden building. You wouldn't notice any difference to an agricultural farm building, only the fact that the southern aspect is equipped with solar collectors.[14]

It houses a storage area for firewood, the boiler and two huge buffer storages both of which have been buried two

---

[14]*Please note: In the southern hemisphere the sun collectors are orientated to the north for maximum exposure).*

thirds into the ground. The water in the tanks is heated by either solar power or burning wood chips and sent hot to the homes and buildings which are connected to the system.

1996 in spring 70 more buildings in the idyllic vine growing village in 'Retzer Becken', Austria, have been connected. This means that 70 old and faulty individual heaters have been replaced by solar panels plus the burning of wood off cuts.

"On nice days, the sun is enough to keep us warm. When the weather is cold and foggy, we burn the wood off cuts collected from local sawmills, carpentries and leftovers from the forest. Over the last years the price for this kind of wood has dropped so low that it is not worthwhile to sell it. Now we make the best use of it by burning it in our heating system and keeping our environment clean and pristine."

Guest and visitors are most welcome to have a good look around the village to find out how localizing the energy supply has empowered this community. The use of gentle energy has a long tradition here. The last active windmill in Austria is as much an example as all the other tourist attractions of this vine growing area which is so very rich in culture and beautiful attractions!

Only a decade later, Biomasseheizungen and wood pellets are vital parts part of the international climate discussions in politics. Burning pellets for heating has led to a drastic lowering of the CO_2 emissions. At the same time forestry framers are achieving better and fairer prices for their wood off cuts and leftovers. In Austria alone there are more Biomasseheizungen being installed every year than oil heaters. May the day come when trees are not being turned into toxic building materials!

Chapter Seven - 'New' ways to live in harmony with nature

- **The voices of science**
- **Regulations, laws and dogmas**
- **A sign post to a positive development?**
- **The mystery of trees**

The voices of science

After we changed our manufacturing process to be absolutely chemical free we decided to only process trees harvested at the right time. Our saw mill received mixed reactions from the scientific community and there were a number of opinions as well as the odd 'doubting Thomas'. However, some scientists agree there is more than just measuring instruments, numbers and formulas at play – something which might best be approached by 'feeling' one's way.

This quotation is from a conversation I had with a famous German physics scientist and author Professor Reinhard Furrer[15] about wood harvested at the right time:

"It would be foolhardy for me to deny phenomena and linkages of things only because it hasn't yet been proven scientifically. Of course I cannot confirm either as long as they haven't been investigated appropriately. However, I myself am a lover of nature. I own a wonderful table which shows a very beautiful grain. This table continues to uplift me when I just sit down and let my hand touch and slide across the top. It actually provides me with a sense of peace and strength. It would be totally untrue if I were to deny the fact that natural materials like wood and stone are providing strength to humans, only because the energy exchange between humans and furniture have not yet been scientifically investigated. History tells us that gut feelings and experiences of ordinary people sometimes have been way ahead of their times. Often scientific proof came quite some time later."

---

[15]Professor Reinhard Furrer *was a famous German physicist and astronaut who, while taking part in a space project, has circumnavigated the earth 120 times. He died in 1995.*

Regulations, laws and dogmas

In the spirit of technical advancement, the relationship between human beings and building materials is defined by numbers and patents. Today many wood workers only work with standards and regulations.

I am not demonizing all norms and regulations here; however, it simply is erroneous and destructive to reduce our relationship with trees to numbers and regulations. Sorting out and grading the quality of building wood by counting the branches of the trees doesn't result in buildings which last for centuries. A practical example is the trade laws, norms and standards which regulate the wood industry. They grade by the exact numbers and size of branches in a board or beam. Our experience however shows that the amount of branches is one of the least criteria which contribute to quality. For our winter gardens and glass facades we fit large glass panels of solid untreated timber beams. Those beams have to be absolutely steady. If there is any movement as through cracking or warping, the glass would shatter. The largest glass panels we ever installed were about 5 meter high thermal glass panels in one piece. These panels still are intact on after many years and have amazed quite a few

It would be extremely difficult for us to achieve the required qualities (like durability and stability) by solely relying on industry norms. These regulations don't say anything about the right selection or the right time for harvesting trees. They do not mention the markedly different qualities of juvenile and mature trees. There is no comparison between wood drying naturally slow and super-fast kiln drying.

We have used beams which have up to 10 cm 'splay knots' to support large glass panels. According to standards these beams are of low grade. However, they have performed perfectly for many years and they will do so for generations to come. Branches are the organs of a tree and are a big part of the wood story.

For the winter garden I could have used an industrial 'high grade' wood without any knots. It could have grown in an unnatural monoculture, harvested while still juvenile, in the middle of a growth spurt and dried fast in a kiln. The wood would have been sprayed against the bark beetle and possibly been dipped into a fungicide. This wood would be perfectly graded and comply with all standards. Nevertheless, I would not use wood that has been so badly mistreated to build a winter garden but be very concerned about the possibility of glass panels breaking, the wood slow resistance to insects and fungi as well as toxic residues.

The tools used to grade wood are simply too primitive when we start working within the natural cycles. Moon calendars, zodiac sign, seasons and the choice of trees are more effective aids for us to befriend nature. However, nature's rules too can be questionable when followed with a very narrow mind. I have met people who swap industry regulations for the 'New Moon Calendar' in the same fanatical way.

Nothing ever benefits by fanaticism, pretension and narrow mindedness. To live in harmony with nature has to do with appreciation and consideration and the same goes for wood.

A sign post to a positive development?

In the early 1980s, forestry death was brought to the attention of the public for the first time. Dire reports predicting there would not be a single tree left standing in Europe took turns with appeasements and playing down the problem.

Nowadays, we are able to look at several studies done by governments and forestry departments. We know about the regional dramatic repercussions, for example in the

'Erz- and Riesengebirge', where whole mountain ranges are bare of trees and are turning into steppe. We also registered tree diseases of particular types such as elm, oak and spruce to name just a few.

On the other hand, most of our forests have survived the catastrophic storms of 1990 (violent storms Vivian and Wiebke) quite well. Forest managers and farmers have learnt much and nowadays, monocultures are rarely being planted anymore in middle Europe.

Is the decline of forest still an issue today? Our technically advanced world, where all decision-making is done by the logical left brain, has tried to capture the phenomena of forest dieback with environmental impact studies, percentages and statistics. However, this is a big mistake which is about as erroneous as the planting of monocultures 20, 50 and 100 years ago.

Imagine your child has measles. The doctor does nothing else but counts all the red spots on your child's skin and records it in a highly bureaucratic way. Would you trust this doctor? It is a similar situation with our forest. Statistics alone will not do the trick.

Every tree is an amazing living being which connects heaven to earth. The plant and animal communities which live in and around trees constitute the forest. The question is when is a tree well? What is the foundation of our wellbeing? The answer is we are feeling well and healthy when we are being loved and able to pass this love on to others. It is well known that people who speak to and touch their plants lovingly have the most beautiful flowers. We can apply this to our forests too and love our woods. We too will be healthier and feel better.

How is 'loving the forest' supposed to look like in our daily life? To love something means to fully integrate it into one's life. The human being or the object of our love must not leave or be banned from our life. And this is where our forests have suffered most ill. Polluted air and bark beetles are only symptoms manifesting what has already happened in the hearts of humanity.

Think about the large herds of bison in the northern America prairies. As long as the local Native Americans loved, appreciated and respectfully treated the animals, both the Indians and the bison were well. This balance lasted over hundreds of years. The bison meat nourished the Indians and the skins gave them a roof over their head. The white settlers brought along their own way of life and didn't understand the bison the way Indians did. Because the bison didn't have a place in the hearts of the white population, it did not take long for the animals to become extinct.

It's not the bark beetle which threatens our forests; it is us who do not cherish it. Insects are as much a part of the forest community like birds, fox or deer are. The real cause for the death of our trees is the idea that we don't need them anymore in our daily life. Once we belief this, we start neglecting the forest.

It becomes more dangerous for the forest, when our children grow up in houses made of toxic materials, plastic instead of wooden furniture and toys. When they don't get to see and feel the magic and beauty of wood grain, wood floors, toys and musical instruments. Girls and boys nowadays grow up playing on synthetic flooring instead of warm wooden surfaces. Children surrounded by reinforced concrete instead of imaginative wood grain will find it difficult to connect with wood in their later life.

Do you remember a wooden object from your childhood, one which you have touched often? Do you remember the floor boards or furniture in your bedroom which you were looking at every day when falling asleep? All the faces and animals and other imaginative beings you saw in its knotholes and grain? Subconsciously we experience our surrounding and mother nature in this manner every day. Can we afford to go without?

When we perceive precious wood in our forests as a cheap resource instead of a divine gift, our forests are in danger. We start clear cutting large areas for profit instead of harvesting mature trees to make space for young ones and give them their chance of developing. Once the wood has been treated, it is toxic and cannot be returned to nature to turn into mulch and provide nutrients for the next generation.

To protect our environment means to accept and use it in a sensible way. Let us provide a healthy environment for our forests and make the best use of this awesome resource. Once wood plays a valuable role in people's lives again and we embrace wood as a divine gift, the forests will be treated best.

The mystery of trees

Life has a better quality to it when we are able to live in homes which have furniture and floors made of natural wood. However, one has to cut down living trees. Is this the right thing to do?

Does the life of a tree start when the seed is sprouting or before, when the oak seed, beech nut or cembra nut or a winged seed falls off the tree? Or even earlier, when the seed is ripening on the mother tree? Maybe even before that, when the genetic information for the upcoming flower and seed production is being determined? Is it possible to say when exactly life begins? Grasping the mystery of trees leads us to many magical natural cycles.

As a living and active being, the tree pioneers into the dark world which we came from and will return to. We try to negate this underworld from our thoughts maybe because it reminds us of our own mortality? Could this be one of the reasons why we don't like to think about death?

By penetrating this underground with its roots, the tree interacts and changes this world. Deeply anchored in the earth's darkest realms, the tree grows its trunk into the opposite element. It carries branches with needles or leaves, flowers and fruit upwards into the sky towards the light of the sun. An exact mirror image to the roots in the soil, the leaves and needles interact with light, air, wind and weather. Trees impact the physical and chemical levels by absorbing carbon monoxide and producing oxygen. It also affects the sensory world of humans, animals and plants by its form, color and sound.

An example of one of the many ways trees interact with their environment is shown by American research regarding the impact sound frequencies of birds have on the development of plant cells. It has been found, that for trees to develop properly, they also need the sound of birds singing!

In this study[16] it was proven that particular plant cells absorb water and nutrients better with the specific sound frequencies of bird songs. Simply put, the sound of birds promotes the growth of plants. Apart from this, there is a huge amount of interconnection between trees and their environment, which simply keeps us short of words.

Who doesn't know the light and liberating feeling of happiness which overcomes us when looking at a flowering cherry tree in spring? The elemental forces touch us when we see how an old oak tree defies a violent autumn storm, when we hear the gentle whisper of Aspen leaves? The language of trees is more beautiful and facetted than anyone could ever put down on paper.

Leaves, needles and branches harness light and the heavenly energies of the sky which then is channeled via the trunk to the roots into the opposite element, the earth. Oxygen, fertility and life reach and penetrate the dark layers of the earth. This energy makes the soil fertile and

---

[16]*Peter Tompkins and Christopher Bird: The Secrets of our Beautiful Earth, Munich 1991.*

helps seeds to sprout and grow towards the light of the sun and the cycle closes.

Every tree naturally transmits light into the darkness of the earth and transforms airy energies into solid form. The sky's energy floods through the tree into the earth, darkness and light complete each other. A tree is much more than a collection of wooden cells or the sequence of biological reactions. A large variety of wonderful cycles, polar opposites, tensions, rhythms are balancing and harmonizing extremes, shrouding trees in mystery. It is this mysterious vitality behind the tree which decides about its life and death.

The death of a tree starts with the destruction of its inherent mystery by wiping out the idea of our natural cycles and the connection between heaven and earth. In many religions and cultures we find trees as symbols for life. As such the tree doesn't die when harvested, but when it's connections, rhythms and tasks are taken away and when it is banned from the lives of humans.

In the book of genesis: *The Lord God made to grow from the soil every tree that is pleasant to sight and good for food. The tree of life and the tree of knowledge grow in the middle of the garden.*

Of what practical value is it for builders and buyers to know about the secret life of trees? From an ecological building point of view, we know that untreated wood is breathing building material; it absorbs, retains and releases moisture. It makes contact with us humans via our senses. We perceive its color, form and the spirit which has worked it.

A piece of furniture or floor can have a calming, uplifting, joyous effect and supply us with energy. It also can be frustrating, worrying and weakening. Crucial here is the question: what has been done to the wood. How was it treated and worked with?

To harvest a tree doesn't mean to kill it. The falling of a mature tree is part of the natural cycle. The decay to humus is the basis of existence for the next generation.

This brings us to the conclusion

Trees are living beings and they connect the divine air element with the earthy, dense and dark energies of the soil. It is possible to work with wood in ways where synthetic chemicals are not needed. Natural wood can last for hundreds of years and after its usage it still can safely be returned to nature. As ash and mulch it provides nutrients for the next generation of trees and the natural cycle closes.

If you are a mother looking for toys for your children, a builder, worker, architect, wood sawyer or forester in the forest, we all can work on this huge task from our points of view. By consciously working with nature, we enrich, enliven and keep her riches for our children. Embracing the gift of our forests is the easy way to bring the mystery of trees into our hearts. Enjoyment, fulfillment and finding our own mystery will be our reward.

Part Three - Information and Service

When are the best days to harvest for building wood? How long should wooden be air-dried before you can turn them it into furniture. Is it necessary to paint the external cladding of the house? Not everyone can ask their grandfather for advice like I could. This book's purpose is to answer your questions and to inspire you to find a new. Making changes is not easy and requires overcoming inertia. So don't expect to get a hug when you turn up at the saw mill with your checklist and questions.

Wood - a very peculiar material

Wood is not homogenous like for example metal, glass or some synthetics. It consists of a variety of ingredients, combination of cells, pores, capillaries and provides a plethora of fantastic characteristics.

You can work out the specific strength of a material by using the 'self-support length' method – the maximum length of a vertical column that can suspend its own weight. For steel, this length depends on the steels quality and is around 2–4 miles. For aluminum it is 6 miles while for wood it is (depending on type and structure) 6–18 miles. The results for wood are excellent when considering the context between volume, its weight and ability to insulate acoustically and thermally.

Expansion and shrinkage of wood

Round wood and freshly sawn boards have higher moisture contents than wooden furniture and wood that has been built with. Wood dries until it has adapted to the surrounding climate and comes to a point where its moisture content hardly varies anymore. This drying process is the reason for a loss of volume, called shrinkage and causes the wood to move in different ways.

Let's have a closer look at shrinkage:

A Future with Natural Wood

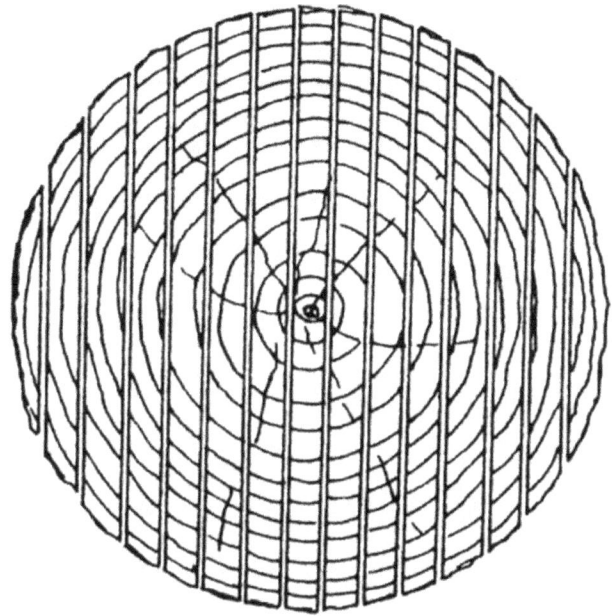

Freshly cut log

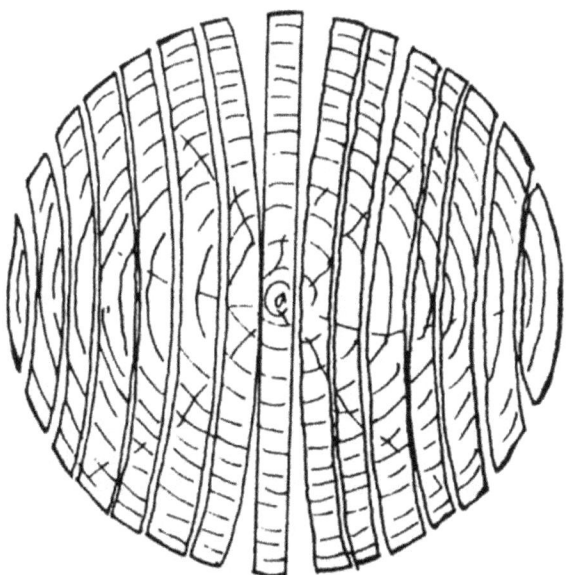

The same log some months or years later:

The older part in the center of the log shrinks less than the younger wood the periphery. With a round log or a stronger piece of squared wood, the outside and younger growth rings hold the inner, older growth rings like staves which keep a barrel together. The tension is rising until its core is cracked by sheer force.

Squared wood free of its heartwood doesn't have this kind of tensions and rarely cracks.

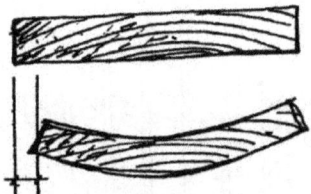

A board with lying growth rings shrinks approximately twice as much (8-10%) and therefore warps more while

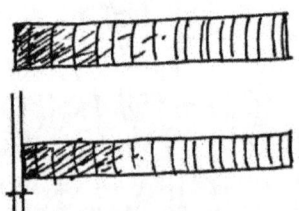

a board with standing growth rings only shrinks about 5 % and hardly warps.

The shrinkage and movement of wood is due to changes in moisture content and are normal. The approach we take towards this natural phenomenon makes all the difference. We can work with wood in a natural way and choose the most suitable tree, harvest it at the right time and allow it to dry naturally to produces a quiet, solid quality wood which doesn't need to be treated!

This poem of an unknown writer is quite fitting here:

The Gap

God created wood, some hard and some soft.
However, one thing is always the same
It will never rest or be inactive.
It will move and work constantly.
Then he bestowed the wood with cells.
So it could shrink and also expand.
But when it was shrinking, it suddenly became clear
There was a gap now.
This is when our wise Lord spoke:
My dear wood, this is how you will be recognized.
Gaps too are part of your nature,
Understand this man, don't try to outsmart me.

Made available by Andreas Scheiblmasser, Baden

Questions you should ask when buying wood

Imagine you want to replace an old carpet with a wooden floor. You would visit a building supply or parquetry distributor where you can chose between different colors, quality and price.

Convenience is often seen as a positive quality and most likely you will be able to take your new laminated flooring material home straight away.

However, do you know where this wood came from? Has it been imported from overseas, the tropics, Russia or the far north? Do you know the components and surface treatment of the laminates? Is your floor releasing toxic fumes? Is this material safely compostable and biodegradable? Can it be burned without being harmful to humans and the environment?

In Europe nowadays, there are wood suppliers who can even give you a photograph of the forest where the wood for your floor has grown. Maybe you would like to see that forest and absorb the environment where your floor came from.

It is best you can treat your floors with natural resins and/or beeswax instead of sealing it with synthetic applications. Then you can be sure that your floor can return to nature and stay in the natural cycle. No matter if you want to buy a bedside table or build a whole family house in wood, to attain the wood quality we are talking about in this book, it is helpful to think about the following questions, before you chose your supplier.

1. The origin of the wood

To transport wood from one continent to the other is affecting our environment and costs energy. You, as a customer want to be sure your wood is not from a radioactive contaminated area (e.g. Chernobyl, Fukushima)! It is important that your wood is from well-managed forests and not from some clear or over felling area where reforestation and appropriate care for the re-growth is not appreciated.

My choice is local wood, because you automatically exclude these risks without having to find out from badly informed suppliers.

2. The age of the trees

Durability and composure are influenced by the maturity of the tree. As a general rule for good wood: coniferous wood should be older than 120 years.

Fast-growing leaf trees like Birch and Alder: older than 50 years; moderate and slow-growing leaf trees like Maple, Ash, Oak and Elm: 100 to 200 years.

These indications are references for high quality workmanship purposes.

3. Potential chemical treatments:

Forest

- Potential spraying of insecticides.

Transport

- Timber transported across the oceans gets fumigated and often is treated preventatively with Timber /Wood preservatives.
- Spar/round wood gets/ Log's get treated when crossing national borders on its way from the forest to the saw mill.

Sawmill

- No fungicide impregnation on sawn wood.
- No wood preservatives at the wood yard.

Processing

- Particularly synthetic adhesives with active ingredients like Formaldehyde and Isocyanate.

Surfaces

- Wooden surfaces should be treated with natural resins, oils and or beeswax instead of synthetic paints and sealants.

If you want to be on the sure side, chose /choose a supplier who confirms in writing that his supplies have not been chemically treated in their manufacturing process.

4. The right choice of wood for the project

It is best to consult a specialist or research on the internet.

Sophisticated wooden buildings require slow and steady grown trees. For heavy traffic areas durability is of importance and hardwoods like beech, oak, and ash are excellent for solid floor boards. Environmentally this is the best choice and it is wise to avoid hardening the surface with laminates and sealants. Outdoors it is best to use naturally weather resistant wood like larch, oak or untreated robinia.

5. Timber harvesting time

Steadiness and durability can be achieved best by harvesting your wood at the right time. Adhere to the following criteria for building and furniture Timber /Wood:

1. The right time of the year – winter.
2. The right phase of the moon – waning moon and new moon, preferably when the moon moves through the zodiac sign of Capricorn.

(See table "Timber Harvesting Days for Excellent Building and Furniture Wood")

6. Is this choice agreeable with your personal taste and health?

Think about which tree best suits and matches you. There is a distinct difference to living on a larch or an oak floor. To choose the right type of wood translates into positive energy, harmony and better quality of your life.

My advice: make this decision when you are in nature and under trees. You will feel which tree has the best effect on you.

7. Once it has fulfilled its purpose, can it be returned to nature?

If the use of chemicals has been consequently avoided, the answer is a positive: "Yes". It can be returned into the natural cycle as mulch or ash and enrich the soil with nutrients for the next generation of trees to grow.

8. Has it been sawn appropriately?

Here are some examples:

For winter gardens use core free and squared pieces. Boards with standing growth rings(edge grain) are best for wooden floors and bathrooms.

Squared timber with core rips easily

Squared timber without core is more stable

Standing growth rings for timber floors in bathrooms

Core free timber for winter gardens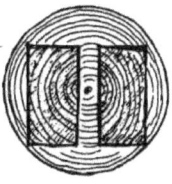

 Top post for balcony railing

Dr. Erwin Thoma

Checklist for buying wood:

The following checklist is meant to help you when buying wood; however the decision depends on your taste and lifestyle. It is just a mnemonic device to make your life easier and not about keeping up with norms and regulations. The time you are putting into research and planning now will save you time and effort later and helps you avoid harm to yourself or your tenant.

Please do not expect to find open doors with all trades people when coming along with your list. Many companies will be overwhelmed.

	Where	When	Which Tree	Age	Storage and Drying Periods
	Do you know where your tree has grown?	Use the right time to harvest	Select trees which have grown slowly	Only use mature trees	Use timber which has been seasoned and stored properly (1-5 years air drying)
Wooden toys	◆	▼			
Furniture	◆	◆	◆	▼	◆
Floors, halls, parquetry	◆	◆	◆	◆	◆
Formwork indoor, lining	◆	◆	▼	◆	◆
Formwork outdoor, cladding	◆	◆	◆	◆	◆
Visible building timber	◆	◆	◆	◆	◆
Hidden building timber,	◆	▼	▼	▼	◆
Winter gardens	◆	◆	◆	◆	◆
Windows, doors	◆	◆	◆	◆	◆
Garden furniture	◆	◆	▼	◆	◆
Outdoors like pergola, verandah, fence etc	◆	◆	◆	◆	◆
Wood for tools like wedges, handles	◆	▼	◆▼	▼	◆
Firewood	◆				◆

◆ Is recommended   ▼ improves results   ● only recommended for areas exposed to weather

A Future with Natural Wood

	Drying	Weathering	Glue	Glue	Color	Processing	Type of Timber
	Slow kiln dry at the end only, to remove rest moisture	Use only suitable timber like Larch, Oak and Robinia	Without any adhesives	Only casein glue in very small quantities	Only natural bees wax, plant oils and resins for surface treatment	Talking with a professional about harvesting and processing according to natural laws	Have you found your personal favorite tree?
Wooden toys			▼	◆	◆		◆
Furniture	◆		▼	◆	◆	▼	◆
Floors, halls, parquetry	◆		◆		◆▼	▼	◆
Formwork indoors, lining	◆		◆		▼	◆	◆
Formwork outdoor, cladding		◆	◆	◆	▼	◆	◆
Visible building timber,		●	◆		▼	◆	◆
Hidden building timber		●	◆		▼	◆	◆
Winter gardens		●	◆		▼	◆	◆
Windows, doors	◆	▼		◆	◆	◆	◆
Garden furniture		◆	▼	◆	◆		◆
Outdoors like pergola, veranda, fence etc		◆	◆		▼	◆	◆
Wood for tools like wedges, handles				◆			◆
Firewood				◆			

◆ Is recommended   ▼ improves results   ● only recommended for areas exposed to weather

The best times for harvesting trees

If you want to use excellent wood for building and furniture, the most important criteria is to work out the right harvesting days:

1. Rule - Winter

Mind you, the biological winter of a tree is not exactly identical with our calendar winter. In the northern hemisphere, the stream of sap slows down and finishes in the last week of August. It begins pulsating through the tree again at the end of January, early February. For trees, the winter lasts from September to January/February. When in doubt, I recommend the months in the depths of winter, which is November until January.

2. Rule - Moon Phase

Every lunar month has 14 days from full moon until new moon when the moon is waning. Traditional records say harvesting in winter closer to new moon is better than closer to full moon.

If you adhere to rules 1 and 2, you will produce high-quality building and furniture wood. For all those who put a strong emphasis on the right zodiac sign, here is rule 3:

3. Rule - Zodiac Sign:

This third rule has been handed down through oral tradition and has not been scientifically proven. For those who want to try it anyway, choose the days with rule 1 and 2 and when the moon is in Capricorn, Virgo or Taurus.

My tip for building wood is the waning moon, close to new moon in Capricorn which falls in the middle of winter, usually around Christmas and New Year.

Recommended times for storage and air drying of wood

Building wood, depending on what is being used for: 1–5 years

Floors, cladding from coniferous wood: 1–2 years

Floors from leaf trees like oak needs longer storage and drying time: 2–4 years

Furniture wood: 1 year per 1 cm wood thickness

When properly used, building wood sometimes can finish its drying process after installation. For example, if it is guaranteed that the beams are aerated from all sides and the build is being protected from rain and snow, beams for a timber ceiling can be used a few months after they have been cut in the saw mill. Before you embark on this, you need to discuss with a professional as working with green wood requires particular skills.

If in doubt, the best solution is to dry building wood naturally to about 20% moisture content before building with it.

Natural wood protection

Working only with natural wood protection has several advantages. Natural wood will provide a healthy and long-lasting usage of buildings and also eliminates expensive and complicated products. Here is an excerpt from a tender brief from an engineer's office:

"The existing wooden balconies have, despite consistent maintenance and treatment with commercial chemical wood preservatives, fully rotted away. The main reason is the disregard of constructive measures to protect the

wood. *It also suggests that chemical wood preservatives do not effectively protect external wood, however, it does turn wood into toxic waste."*

In addition, this brief went on to prescribe the demolition and the expensive disposal of the toxic waste. The newly erected balconies were made of alpine larch which has been harvested at the right season and moon phase.

The homeowner could have saved a lot of money had he used natural wood preservation methods along with good quality wood.

What actually do we need to protect our wood from?

When a tree dies, falls and begins to decay, insects, fungi and microorganisms are there to help break down the bark, wood, leaves and needles to return it to the soil where it came from. A healthy forest recycles and reuses everything by turning it into fertile mulch. The next generation of trees is metabolizing the energy of the old trees and keeps the cycle going.

Is it wise to replace natural organisms with chemicals and fight them with poisonous sprays? Or is it more productive to investigate and study the life of fungi and insects? Understanding natural organisms would help us find simple ways to keep them from breaking down our buildings and furniture. If we use common sense, we don't need to poison our surroundings.

When exactly is wood breaking down? 99% of the break down occurs in the forest, under the open sky and exposure to the weather. Our houses all have a protective roof which means that when we cover our build with a roof, the wood stays dry, unlike in a forest.

Insects are of no real threat to good quality wood either. Only very few are able and interested in feeding on dried wood. If we manage to handle this small group of insects naturally, we don't need to treat wood.

The key to those specialized fungi and insects lies in the moisture content of the wood. Building constructively allows us to use naturally dried wood in specific ways so even beetles and fungi will not cause any harm.

Natural wood preservation to prevent fungi

In this table you can see the ideal moisture content which fungi need to grow to decompose wood.

Type of Fungus	Minimum Moisture	Optimum Moisture
Serpula Lacrimans	Arrpox. 20%	30%
Oniphoraputeana	20%	50-60%
Gleophyum Arten	20%	40-60%
Poria Arten	20%	40%
Ascomyceten	30%	30-40%

Table: Bernhard Leisse: Treating Timber Naturally, Heidelberg 1994

Like all living organisms, fungi too look for the best possible conditions and prefer to take the way of least resistance. These optimum living conditions however are not around 20% but rather around 30% moisture content.

When boards, squared timber or slabs are being stacked, covered and stored outside for air drying, the wood ends up with a moisture content of approximately 12-20% (depending on the climatic conditions).When further processed, no matter whether it turns into a piece of furniture, floor, walls or roof, the wood dries out even more.

The moisture content of external wall cladding is around 12-18% (depending on the atmospheric conditions). Indoors, wood in a heated room ends up containing around

6-10% moisture. Basically any wood in the building industry (apart from balconies and terraces) which is protected by a roof is just not moist enough for fungi to exist and grow. Furthermore it is very rare that even wood with 20-25% wood moisture content is infested by destructive fungi.

The proper storage and drying of wood is an important step to prevent it from rot and decay.

The conclusion is, no fungus can grow under 20% moisture content. If we dry wood properly there is no need to use chemicals to protect it from fungi and insects.

The two things which we need to adhere to are:

It would be worth writing a whole book specifically about proper construction methods. Here are some worthwhile recommendations which should be followed by you, the architect, biological building officer and trades people.

1. Protect the building materials and construction from rain and moisture. Avoid lengthy exposure to the weather and finish the roof quickly.

Use well-seasoned Timber / Wood.

A wide enough roof overhang prevents direct contact with rain and is more effective than treatments. Old, wooden buildings always have a wide roof overhang to protect external walls and cladding.

Dr. Erwin Thoma

Keep wood off the moist earth. Cladding and posts should never end up in the ground or soil. Make sure you build on sufficient foundation made from brick, concrete or rock.

Plinth for wooden post

Foundation made from rocks

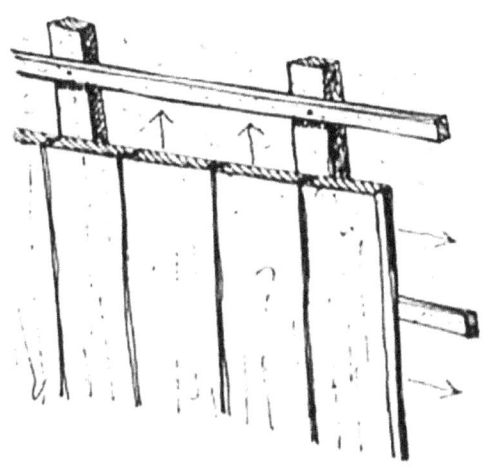

Back ventilation of vertical weather boarding

For an external cladding the vertical façade is preferable to horizontal. Water can run off all the wooden components which are exposed to rain and dampness and doesn't pool.

Weather boards are to be installed onto a slatted frame allowing free air movement and circulation to wooden building components.

Condensation, Frost and Foils:

To build a more energy efficient home, more and better thermal insulation is in demand. However proper insulation needs to dam and should not seal. Avoid water and air tight foils (vapor barriers) and rather use a recommended vapor retardant instead of a barrier.

Condensation and dew water still remain risky for wood frame walls.

It is important to ask professional trade's people about all types of insulation. Ask them to calculate the dew point for every ceiling and wall construction and to confirm their results in writing. At a later point a vapor retardant might get injured and cause damage. The best solution is a solid, homogenous wooden wall like the Holz 100 system presents. Here the vapor pressure is continuously slowed down instead of suppressed by a single, vulnerable layer of foil and guarantees 100% protection from condensation moisture and fungus.

To constructively protect your build, you need a trade person who appreciates this type of work. Luckily those crafts people do exist and their numbers are rising.

2) Be aware of water transportation by dry rot:

There is only one, very rare exemption which can infest even very dry wood. The true dry rot needs damp wood (more than 20%) to grow, however, once established it can grow several meters long in up to one centimeter thick strands. These strands transport water to neighboring, dry areas and dampen these for the infestation to spread.

How to prevent dry rot? If the house has been built in a constructive and proper way, it usually is enough to make sure there are no rotting piles of wood, old building parts or off cuts which provide feeding and breeding ground anywhere close to the building.

When restoring the building, all infested wooden components should be generously removed and any existing strands of fungi should be eliminated from the masonry, brick and stone work with a blowtorch.

Realistically, in all the years of our professional building work, we never came across any dry rot in wood which has been dried, stored and worked with properly.

Natural wood protection against insects

Here the situation is similar, a dry and protected build doesn't offer any chances of survival to most insects. There are only three specialists for dry wood:

Living conditions for the most common and destructive wood insects:

Insect	Optimum Moisture	Temperature
Common Powder Beetle (Lyctus brunneus)	9-60%	11-13 Celsius
Common House Borer (Anobium punctatum)	12-50%	14-29 Celsius
House Longhorn Beetle (Hylotrupes bajulus) Infests cConifers	7-28%	Up to 32 Celsius

Table: Bernhard Leisse: Treating Wood naturally, Heidelberg 1994

Only those three species are able to live in dry conditions. At first this appears as a danger to anything made with wood. But only at first glance! Let us have a closer look at why constructive building methods have defied this trio for hundreds of years:

Common Powderpost Beetle

The Common Powderpost Beetle is not native to Europe; most likely it was introduced with imported wood from the tropics. Even though it is able to infest dry wood in our cold climate, it doesn't feel at ease here. It doesn't enjoy the European species of trees. It doesn't like conifers at all and only the light colored types of leafy trees (like maple) or the periphery of some trunks are edible. In the northern hemisphere, this tropical migrant can't fly from one home to the next; therefore, new infestation is hardly possible.

You can treat a contaminated piece of furniture effectively by putting it outside on a frosty night and all beetles and eggs will be destroyed. Therefore, this exotic creature does not really pose any threat to buildings and furniture made of spruce, pine, fir or larch.

Common House Borer and Knock Beetle

These beetles are able to survive in wood with moisture content as low as 12 %, their optimum however lies around 30%. In heated rooms with a wood moisture around 6% to 12% it simply cannot exist.

It mostly spreads when damp or infected wood has been used. By thoroughly drying and aerating stored wood and only using wood free of infestations, you can reduce the danger of the House Borer or Knock Beetle to just about zero.

In case treatment is necessary, heat treatment is very successful (look at the House Longhorn Beetle).

House Longhorn Beetle

The Longhorn Beetle is the most significant of all the damaging insects. If we use reasonable caution and constructive measures when building with wood, it does not pose a real danger to our buildings.

It only attacks conifers and not hardwood and needs small cracks and tears to deposit its eggs. Dressed beams make it very hard for it to breed. It is very territorial and in towns where it is unknown, it is unlikely to just appear. Speak to local carpenters and wood workers to find out if there are any known infestations in your area.

It is best to use wood which has been harvested at the right time. Treat all wooden components before installing them with a boric salt preparation. Boric salt is a naturally occurring substance and is classed as harmless in the ecological building industry.

Nutrients are attractive to insects and when wood is aging, protein and carbohydrates are broken down, leaving 30 – 50 year old buildings immune to infestation. It is important therefore to allow wood to season slowly and naturally before working with it.

Risk of infestation by Longhorn Beetles in context to the age of the wood:

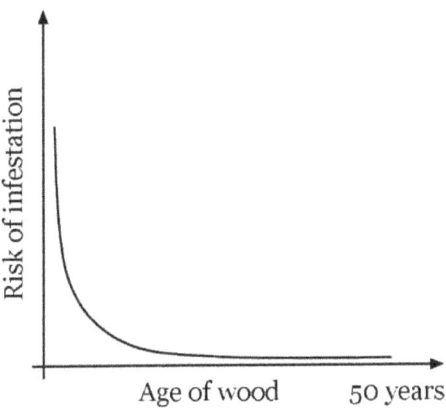

The table shows that the older the Timber / Wood the less likely it will be attacked by the Longhorn Beetle.

Should the Longhorn Beetle have established itself, there is still no need to panic! If you heat up the infested parts (right into the core of the wood) for more than three hours and above 55 C, all insect life dies! Smaller pieces like furniture can be put into the sauna or a kiln for treatment. Infested roof trusses and wooden houses can be treated with hot air by specialized companies for the same effect. A re-infestation in older wood is practically impossible.

If we choose appropriately, harvest at the right time, season wood properly and use constructive building methods, chemical treatments become redundant. The oldest preserved dwellings are solely built with stone and untreated wood and have survived for millennia.

Timber constructions outdoors

Nature intended wood to weather and finally break down into mulch to close the natural cycle. It is an illusion to think it could last forever when exposed to wind and weather on a daily basis. Nevertheless, there are natural ways we can use to make wood last considerably longer. Some woods like Douglas fir and Larch, disintegrate much slower than other species such as Spruce and Pine. Additionally to carefully selecting weatherproof and long lasting woods, we can use particular building techniques which further delay the decaying process.

Here are some examples:

A wooden deck outdoors built with fast grown Spruce and Pine (harvested in spring or summer) and with water pooling on it, can easily break down after just three years.

Whereas a deck built with alpine Spruce that was harvested at the right time and installed constructively, lasts for 30 years or longer. The same decking made with sapwood free oak is more expensive but will last 50 years or longer!

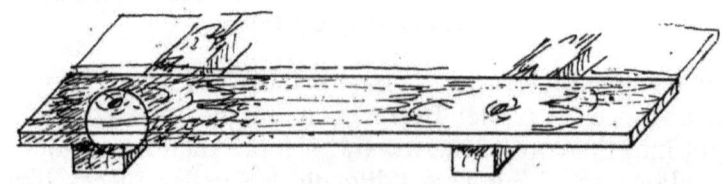

Water pooling on horizontal wooden surface, halves its life expectancy.

The screw heads often rip into the wooden fibers at the surface and cause small puddles of water. These boards will rot twice as fast. Ideally it is best to screw from underneath. It is also better to divide the deck area into segments and then place them on the structural elements without screws. The same principle works for balconies and all other similar constructions.

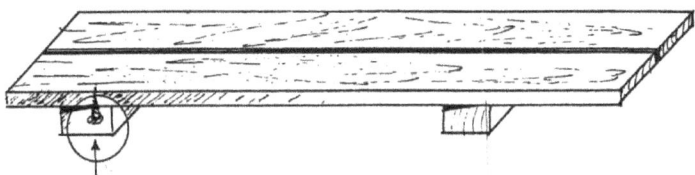

Sleepers should be chamfered so that moisture can run off. It is best for the decking to lie on wedges which are narrower than the boards themselves. The verandah should have a slight slope, for the water to run off.

For outdoor constructions, avoid building exact horizontal areas and use some simple practices in combination with the right selection of wood.

Balcony railing details.

Sloped cross members of wooden fences are more effective than any product applied on an otherwise badly built fence. Good practice extends the lifespan for a considerable amount of time.

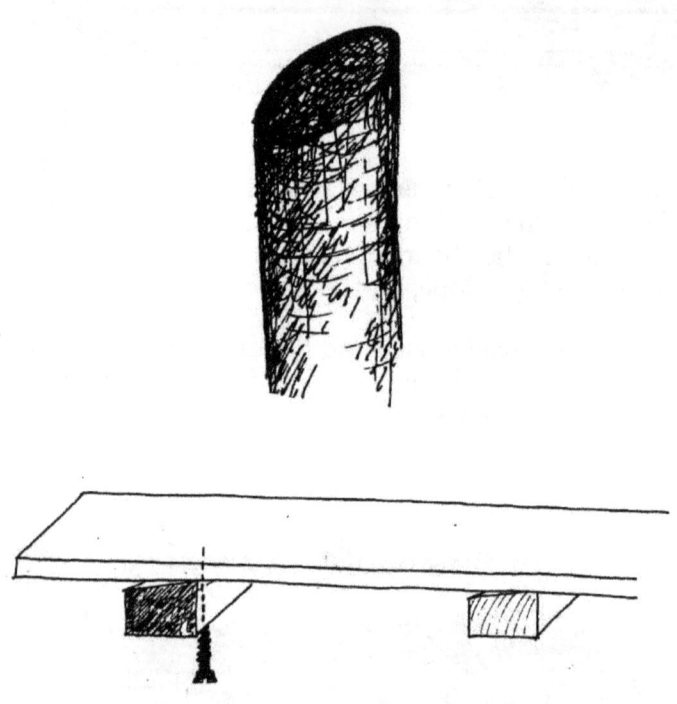

Screwed diagonally from underneath

If you cannot relinquish a level surface, it is best to fix a board with standing growth rings from below.

Maintenance and care for wood

Hardly any other building material has been as wrongly judged to be high maintenance as wood has been. However, no other building material has been treated with such harmful products, some extremely poisonous. This leaves many people unsure of how to maintain wooden surfaces effectively.

Maintenance and care for wood

Purpose	Prolongs longevity and function	For easy maintenance	Not necessary, just for optical reasons
Wooden toys		▼	▼
Furniture		♦	
Floors		♦	
Formwork, inside lining		▼	
Formwork, outside lining	▼		▼
Timber covered by roof			♦
Wooden ceiling		▼	♦
Winter gardens			♦
Windows	♦		
Doors		♦	
Garden furniture	▼		
Outdoors like pergola, verandah, fence etc.	▼		▼
Wood for tools like wedges, handles			♦

♦ Is recommended   ▼ is not necessary, however it improves results

If you want to fully enjoy living with wood, it is important to only use natural paint products or leave it completely untreated.

Natural paints derived from plant-derived oils, resins, natural waxes and minerals consist of substances which appear in nature. Buy only paints and products where the manufacturer lists all ingredients used. A quality wood coating is meant to allow the wood to breath and not seal its pores. In this way, you can enjoy your wood product not only visually, but also its ambience and moisture-balancing properties.

Sun and wood

This is mainly an issue with wood on external surfaces like cladding. Indoors, the sun only leaves a few small discolorations and has little impact on wood.

Can you imagine, if all humans had the same skin and hair color? Luckily this isn't the case. We also ask our children to have respect for our white haired elders. The wrinkles and grooves in old people's faces are wonderful and honest witnesses to their trials and triumphs.

As children, we often sat next to our granddad and our delicate hands would touch the protruding veins on his old hands. It was a fun game to squeeze his hands for a moment and watch how his blood streamed back into the veins and filled them up again. It would be strange to think that after all those years working as a carpenter his hands should have remained with the same skin color as our youthful hands.

Why then, do we expect the skin of our wooden buildings to always look young and new? Why do we demand that a building needs to be the same yellow or brown color from every angle at all times? The life expectancy of a wooden dwelling has little to do with paint and paint brush and traditionally, wooden buildings never saw a coat of paint. Most people nowadays don't hesitate and apply a coating to seal any wooden surface thinking they are preserving the wood. However, just a few years later they are faced with paint peeling off and wood rot underneath.

1. The suns weathering impact:

Ultraviolet (UV) light generally causes just a light deterioration of wood. This breaking down process however is very slow and it takes centauries for deep traces to show up. It is not necessary to protect the wood surfaces of a well-built wood dwelling with a coat of paint against the sun. We recommend a coat of natural paint only for wooden windows. The often heard statement that pigments do protect from sunlight is basically correct. However, what is not being mentioned is that wood by itself finds the best and most suitable color. If the painted color is too light it doesn't protect from the sun. If it is too dark, the wood absorbs too much heat.

You probably have occasionally worn dark clothing on a hot summer's day and were melting in the sun? If so, you can empathize with an external wood cladding which has been painted in dark colors and now absorbs the heat. High temperature variations during day and night cause cracks in the paint and destroy its protective effect.

The clue is that over the years, wood produces a superior protective layer all by itself. Sunlight shines onto the different sides of the building and causes the wood to adapt with the most appropriate and protective shade. Old wooden buildings have survived for centauries without having been painted at all.

You can observe a different tone of color on every elevation of the building, as varied as nature herself. Why are we so unimaginative and insist that all walls of our buildings have to be the same color?

2. Visual changes caused by the sun:

It is not the purpose to discuss taste and fashion here. Nevertheless, I would like to offer some thoughts which might give you another point of view for your building project.

When landscape photographers want to convey beauty and harmony they often take photos of old buildings which have never seen a coat of paint. Façades which show creases and colorations tell their own stories and observers feel the harmony between building and surrounding.

We visit open air museums and enthusiastically admire suntanned building facades. Then we drive through the countryside and look at the facades of new buildings. We should ask ourselves: "Where are all the people who love and enjoy those old wooden buildings with so much patina and character?"

Why are there so few architects and builders with the courage to let their buildings be colored by the sun and weather? Money cannot be the reason here - because the sun works for free.

Before you consider painting ask yourself this question: "Did I consider the overall costs for work, material and the continuous upkeep?" When building properly and omitting construction mistakes, you will save all these costs. However, buildings which have been designed and built poorly cannot be maintained for long with or without more paint.

If you cannot see yourself happy with natural coloration caused by the sun and you still want to paint it, avoid using paints which harm you and the environment. There are quality natural paints available and you recognize trustworthy natural paint manufacturers by their willingness to provide a listing with all the paints ingredients.

Rough sawn or dressed?

This question often comes up in the context of UV protection and weathering:

"Should wooden surfaces outdoors be dressed or stay rough sawn?"

Arguments for a dressed surface:

- Water runs off better when the surface is smooth and Wood dries faster.
- The area where hands come into contact with wood (external cladding on ground level, balconies) is safer when dressed because there is no splintering.
- In case it will be painted, dressed wood needs less paint.
- Optical reasons and taste.

One opinion is that rough sawn wood is more favorable for insects to lay eggs on, compared to dressed wood.

Adequate protection from insects is mainly achieved by:

- The right choice of wood type and mature tree
- The right time of harvesting
- Natural drying and proper storage
- Using constructive ways of working with wood
- Making sure the wood stays dry.

Arguments for rough sawn siding, external cladding:

- Less expensive, because all the dressing procedure falls away
- Less use of wood
- Optical reasons and tastes.

Networking

After our small saw mill began to adopt wood-working methods in harmony with nature's seasonal cycles, more and more people supported us in many different ways. Amazement, joy and gratitude is resulting into a steadily growing network. If you would like to contribute your personal experience or interesting story about 'Living with Timber', please send your contribution to:

Iris Detenhoff
Moontime Diary
PO Box 1200
Mullumbimby, NSW 2482
Australia
moontimeoffice@gmail.com

or

Ing. Erwin Thoma
Hasling 35
5622 Goldegg
Austria
info@thoma.at

For more information, please visit

        www.thoma.com.at
        www.moontimediary.com.au

Thank you

Every coincident has a meaning. It is wonderful to recognize, that very often one meets just the right person at the exact right time. Suddenly, without looking, they are there. Without the knowledge, help and goodwill of these people, this book wouldn't be in your hands right now. I want to thank all who supported my writing efforts and also those who act kindly towards Mother Nature. Thank you to the universe for the knowledge and strength which I am allowed to pass on in this way.

Special thanks to my wife Karin and my children for their understanding, patience and contributions; to our Urliopa Gottlieb Brugger for passing on his wisdom and experience, Urlioma Elisabeth, Grandma and Grandpa Hilde; Hans Dabernig; the story telling Mama and Grandma Irene Thoma and many others.

Last not least my heartfelt thanks to Iris Detenhoff who translated this, my first book into English and Gordon Pierce for his foreword. I am very grateful and excited about this dream coming true.

The author's epilogue to this edition

Dear Reader,

While I was writing this book, I didn't anticipate the overwhelming appreciation and rising awareness towards sustainable forestry management and the influence of the moon. My passion is to build solid wooden homes which are (technically and scientifically measurably) superior in all building disciplines and regulations to conventional homes.

To make this vision reality I have founded a Scientific Research Centre in Goldegg where we test and investigate traditional 'Moon Timber' and building methods. We are finding extraordinary evidence for its longevity and have

Dr. Erwin Thoma

been able to develop and patent our Holz 100 System which consists of prefabricated 100% natural wood elements.

With this system we achieved:

- A world record in thermal insulation of any structural building products.
- A 5 times better fire safety ratings than conventional buildings.
- A 99.9% effective barrier to electromagnetic radiation, e.g. cell phones, microwaves etc.
- Natural cooling effect in summer months and warming effect in winter.
- Minimal room temperature fluctuations due to the slow cooling down (Thermal Mass) of the wooden walls.
- Up to 3500 heart beats less per day (wood soothes the heart).
- A dream atmosphere for allergic and sensitive people.

At first glance these improvements and possibilities are nearly unbelievable.

We combined our ancestors' traditional methods with modern technology and found the solutions needed in the 21 century.

Cordially yours,

Erwin Thoma,

Goldegg

www.ingramcontent.com/pod-product-compliance
Lightning Source LLC
Chambersburg PA
CBHW031433150426
43191CB00006B/501